Healthy Mindset for Athletes & Workplace Athletes

Helping Athletes Achieve Their Dreams and Goals While Being Mindful of Everything in Life!

By

Mike Hartman

Table of Contents

Introduction

I was never supposed to make it.

I was too short and too small and made up for it by being too slow. Everyone agreed there was absolutely no way I would ever become a professional hockey player.

Everyone agreed, that is, except for me. I believed, and because I believed, I made believers out of my family, friends, coaches, and eventual teammates.

I believed, and I worked. I believed, and I sweated. I believed, and I learned. I believed, and I planned. I believed and worked, sweated, learned and planned even more.

Some people would see my situation and give up. I lived my situation and used the inadequacies people saw as fuel to make myself better. I'd prove to them I had what it took.

Because I would not give up, because I worked hard and because I made the most out of what talent I did have, I achieved my personal best. I became a professional hockey player in the National Hockey League.

I made it. And so can you.

Growing up in Oak Park, a small suburb of Detroit, Michigan, I knew from an early age that I loved one activity over any other. From the first time I watched one of the older neighbor boys strap on his skates and pick up his well-worn wooden hockey stick, I knew hockey would be a driving force in my life.

Fortunately for me, I came from an athletic family. My dad, who owned a wallpaper store, had played sports for most of his youth growing up and was a photographer for the Detroit Red Wings hockey team. My mom, who didn't work outside the house, was a fantastic athlete. Growing up, she had been an excellent sprinter and baseball player.

Although I didn't know it then, I was fortunate. Because my parents knew what it was like to fall in love with and excel in a sport, they were more accommodating of my desire to play hockey than they might have been.

I wanted to join the Oak Park Rangers, the local house league team. The house league was a community hockey league full of local kids from the neighborhood, coached by parents and featuring what could only barely be called hockey because it was played on ice with sticks.

The Oak Park house league was about as far away from the National Hockey League as possible, but it was where I could start. I battered my parents again and again. I knew I could play.

Over the years I played in the house league, I can't count the number of times I got knocked down or run over. But each time I got knocked down, I got right back up, determined that it wasn't going to happen again. My coaches worried my small size would make it impossible for me to play effectively, but I saw it as a plus.

Because I didn't have the size and strength a lot of the other kids did, I found myself burning with a fire to prove myself every time I strapped on my skates. I made myself skate harder, skate faster and play harder every day. I made the willpower I would need to get better. I focused on doing the best I could in school, even though I didn't like homework because my parents stressed the importance of education. They were right.

The first time I tried out for a travel hockey team, I didn't make it. I wasn't good enough yet. But then my dad said something that changed my life.

"When you try out the next time, you'll just need to make sure your best is even better than it was today. That's all."

I know some people might have taken the failed tryout as a sign that they should give up hockey (or baseball, or basketball, or football, or making the quiz team in school), but I couldn't. I love hockey. I wasn't going to give it up. I wasn't going to give up my dream of becoming a player in the National Hockey League.

I had to get better. By the time my dad and I got home, I was more determined than ever to achieve my goal. I would dedicate myself to improving my game.

The thing was, though, before I could improve, I needed to know what to improve. For that, I looked to the coach's evaluation. He had some specific issues with my game. Even though it hurt to remember what he said when he cut me from the travel team, the coach knew what he was talking about. He certainly knew more than I did, so I needed to take his advice and apply it to my life. His words formed the basis for my hockey-improvement plan.

That was one of the hardest lessons I had to learn. Even when I didn't want to hear someone tell me I wasn't good enough, I had to be strong enough and mature enough to listen to what was said and use that advice to improve my performance.

Throughout my career in the NHL and, really, in all of hockey, I was never a finesse player. I was known as a hard, physical player, someone who was more of a grinder or a digger than what's known as a skill player. But I didn't mind that. I was okay with that. I knew my strengths and weaknesses very well and decided to work within them to improve them. I saw what I was good at and tried to get better. I listened to my coaches to find my challenge areas and worked to reduce those areas or turn them into strengths. That's what enabled me to make it to the NHL.

The secret to my success as a player then and as a coach now is that I found what I was good at – being a hard worker, someone willing to do anything and do it at top speed at any time – and applied those strengths to help my team win. Before you can contribute to a winning team, you have to find the one thing you do very well.

Never give up on your dreams, and never, ever expect that the journey you'll take on the way to achieving those dreams will be easy. It's the difficulty that makes achieving that dream all the more worthwhile.

I can't imagine how empty I would feel if I had given up on my dreams. The ache of unfulfilled dreams must surely be the worst pain of all. The pain of a twisted ankle barely able to fit into a skate is nothing compared to what I would have felt had I given up on my dream of playing in the NHL.

There are millions of different dreams in the world and millions of different paths to finding fulfillment, but there is only one way to get to these different destinations. You need to find something you love, something you're passionate about and then work your hardest to get there.

Most important of all, though, is to remember to have fun on your way. If you enjoy yourself on the way to your goal, it will be all the sweeter when you achieve it.

Achieving your personal best isn't something you can do over the course of an hour or a week, or even a month. It takes long hours, a great plan and the dedication to see it through. It takes establishing a healthy mindset and taking the time to learn everything you can about what it is you're trying to achieve. It takes making a commitment to improving every day, no matter how small the improvement may be. Most importantly, it takes believing in yourself even when everyone else says it's impossible.

Throughout my career as a professional hockey player, I benefited from having great coaches and mentors. Combined with my strong drive to improve my game no matter what it took, these coaches and mentors were able to make me a better hockey player and a better man. Once I retired from hockey, I started looking around for a fulfilling career to take the place of professional sports. That's when I realized I had a real obligation to pay forward the incredible guidance I received when I was growing up and during my career.

One of the most important things I learned while growing up is that it's very important to have a plan. You need to talk with mentors, friends, family and others with knowledge of your goals to get all the information you can. Once you have your information, you can break it down into achievable steps that will lead to your goal.

A lot of people say that life is a marathon; you keep running and running, having to hoard your energy for the hard work just down the line. I don't believe that. Life is a series of short sprints, and it's all about recovering energy between those sprints. That rest and recovery are what give you the energy to run flat-out as fast and as good as you can during the next sprint.

If you're running a marathon, in the end, you're exhausted and have nothing left to give. In a sprint, you can focus on that sprint and give everything you've got, with no worry about saving something for later because you know you'll be able to rest and recover when the sprint is over. Put together enough winning sprints, and you'll have run that marathon, but you'll have run harder and stronger than the person who never stopped but never ran as hard as he could.

When I finished playing professional hockey, I became a performance mindset coach to try and help other people achieve their dreams. I've been fortunate that I was able to play with and learn from some of the best leaders and players in the National Hockey League and throughout my hockey career. Everything I learned as a hockey player, I've taken and applied to my calling as a performance mindset coach.

I established Hartman.Academy to work with athletes, coaches and anyone who wants to get better at what they do. I realized quickly that people who were not involved in sports still could benefit from the lessons I'd already learned in hockey and in life.

This workbook combines lessons learned from mentors, coaches and players, along with observations and insight gained through talking with folks through the years. It will help you establish a plan to work towards achieving your personal best and realizing your dreams. No matter what your goal is, big or small, you need a plan and the dedication to see it through.

Chapter 1: The Importance of a Healthy Mindset

Mindfulness for athletes is an important practice to have. This workbook will help you understand mindfulness and how it can help improve your athletic performance whether you are a student-athlete, a workplace athlete, or someone who just likes to stay in shape. Athletes often face a lot of stress, both physically and mentally. Mindfulness can help them learn how to deal with this stress in a healthy way and improve their overall performance.

As you move through the workbook, take your time to understand each concept and answer the questions thoughtfully. Each chapter builds on the last, and by the end, you will have a mindfulness plan to put into action.

Mindfulness can help athletes in many different ways. It can improve focus, concentration, and mental clarity.

What is mindfulness?

Mindfulness is a concept that many athletes have embraced in recent years. This practice, which involves paying close attention to all aspects of the present moment, has been shown to improve performance and reduce stress. By tuning into your physical sensations, thoughts, and emotions in a nonjudgmental way, you can learn to be more present and focused on your training. This, in turn, can help you get more out of your workouts and achieve even greater levels of athletic success. Whether you're just starting out or looking to reach the next level, becoming skilled at mindfulness can be a powerful tool for any athlete.

Why is a healthy mindset important for athletes?

A healthy mindset can help athletes in many different ways. It can improve focus, concentration, and mental clarity. For example, if an athlete is feeling anxious before a big race, mindfulness can help them calm their mind and focus on the task at hand. Additionally, a healthy mindset has been shown to reduce stress levels and improve sleep quality, both of which are important for peak performance.

While there are many benefits to a healthy mindset, it's important to remember that it is a practice that takes time and effort to master. Like anything else, the more you commit to it, the better your results will be. With patience and practice, you can learn how to use mindfulness to enhance your athletic performance.

How can I start practicing mindfulness?

If you're new to mindfulness, there are many ways to get started. One easy way is to simply pay attention to your breath. As you inhale and exhale, focus on the sensations of your breath moving in and out of your body. If your mind starts to wander, simply bring your attention back to your breath. You can also try other healthy mindset exercises, such as walking meditations.

Dr. Scott Greenapple has been in private practice since 1986. He has been involved with Sports Medicine and Injury prevention for over 30 years. He is a six-time member of the U.S. medical staff for Triathlon and Duathlon and has traveled and treated at the World Championships in Europe, and the U.S. Dr. Greenapple has worked with all sports at the highest level with the NFL, NBA, PGA, WNBA, NHL, MLB, Olympic Gold Medalists, Collegiate, High School and Youth athletes.

According to Greenapple, "Mindfulness by definition is paying attention on purpose with intention and attention without judgment. The key is to just be aware, becoming comfortable with being uncomfortable and training the mind to be less reactive with its negativity bias, learning to let go and begin again without judgment. The brain is malleable. It can be re-wired and trained. This is called neuroplasticity. What you practice grows stronger."

He continued, "The use of the breath is a good and easy way to begin. You always have the breath with you, and you have been breathing all your life, so this is an easy anchor to start with. Just focus on the inhale and then the exhale. It only takes 1-3 focused breaths to change the patterns of your thoughts and your responses" (Greenapple, 2022).

Throughout this workbook, there are exercises to guide you in finding the ways to achieve a healthy mindset, not just as an athlete, but as a student, an employee, a child, a parent, and through all walks of life.

What are the benefits of practicing mindfulness?

Mindfulness has been shown to improve focus, concentration, and mental clarity. Additionally, mindfulness has been shown to reduce stress levels and improve sleep quality, both of which are important for peak performance. Some other benefits of mindfulness include increased self-awareness, decreased negative thinking, improved relationships, and enhanced well-being. With regular practice, you can experience these benefits and more.

Improved Focus

Any athlete knows that there are a lot of mental games that go along with physical training. Learning how to focus and block out distractions is a key part of becoming a successful athlete. When athletes are able to focus on the present moment, they can better utilize their energy and resources. They're also less likely to be sidetracked by outside factors that could impact their performance.

For example, if an athlete is worrying about the outcome of a race, they're not going to be as focused on their breathing or their stride. However, if they're able to focus on the present moment and stay in the moment, they'll be more likely to have a successful race. Mental toughness is an essential part of being a successful athlete, and it all starts with learning how to focus on the present moment.

Golfer Tiger Woods is known for his focus. He has faced a lot of adversity throughout his career, but he has always been able to stay focused on his goals. In fact, after winning the 2019 Masters Tournament, Tiger credited his focus and discipline for his victory. Although he hadn't had a great season, he kept telling himself that it wasn't over yet. In an interview after his win, he kept stating that he just focused on the fact that the tournament wasn't over yet, even on the 18th hole.

If you want to be a successful athlete, learning how to focus is essential. And mindfulness can help you do just that.

Improved Concentration

Having a healthy mind is a key skill for athletes both on and off the field. By cultivating an ability to concentrate on the task at hand, athletes can better manage distractions and stay focused during training. This is essential for reaching peak performance and avoiding injury. Moreover, having an awareness of one's own body and mind helps athletes to anticipate challenges before they occur, strengthening their ability to react to difficult situations quickly.

Kevin Durant is an NBA player for the Golden State Warriors. He has won two NBA Finals MVP Awards, four NBA scoring titles, one NBA Most Valuable Player Award, and two Olympic gold medals.

As a professional athlete, Durant has to be able to concentrate on the task at hand. If he isn't focused, he could make a mistake that could cost his team the game. Mistakes are costly in the NBA, and players have to be able to focus on the task at hand in order to avoid them.

In an interview, Durant spoke about how important concentration is for him as a professional athlete. He said, "I think concentration is key in anything you do in life, whether it's playing basketball or just living day-to-day. If you can control your thoughts and really focus on what's important, I think you'll be successful."

As an athlete, if you want to be successful, you need to learn how to concentrate. Mindfulness can help you do just that.

Improved Mental Clarity

In order for athletes to perform at their best, they need to have mental clarity. This means being able to focus on the task at hand and not letting outside distractions or thoughts impact their performance. When an athlete is able to maintain mental clarity, they are able to enter "the zone" where they are completely focused on the task at hand and are able to block out all other distractions. This allows them to perform at their highest level and achieve peak performance. There are a number of techniques that athletes can use to help them maintain mental clarity, such as visualization, positive self-talk, and breathing exercises. By using these techniques, athletes can ensure that they are able to stay focused and perform at their best.

One professional athlete who is known for his mental clarity is LeBron James. He has played for the Cleveland Cavaliers and Miami Heat. He is a three-time NBA champion, four-time NBA MVP, and two-time Olympic gold medalist.

Known as one of the greatest players in the NBA, LeBron James is a master of mental clarity. He is able to block out all distractions and focus on the task at hand. This allows him to perform at his highest level and achieve peak performance. In order to maintain mental clarity, LeBron uses a number of techniques, such as visualization, positive self-talk, and breathing exercises.

With so many benefits to mindfulness, it's no wonder that so many coaches around the world encourage their athletes to incorporate this powerful strategy into their training.

Phil Jackson, known for his work with the Chicago Bulls and Los Angeles Lakers, is a firm believer in the power of a healthy mind, and he has seen first-hand how it can help athletes perform at their best. In an interview, he said, "I think mindfulness is probably the most important thing that any human being can do to develop his or her full potential."

Jackson isn't the only one who believes in the power of a healthy mind. More and more coaches are beginning to see the benefits of incorporating this practice into their athlete's training. As the evidence continues to mount, there is no doubt that mindfulness will continue to gain popularity among athletes and coaches alike.

Lowered Stress and Improved Performance

A healthy mind can help athletes deal with stress and improve performance in a number of ways. First, having a healthy mind can help athletes to stay focused on the task at hand. By practicing mindfulness, athletes learn how to concentrate and block out distractions. This allows them to stay focused and perform at their best.

Increased Self-Awareness

Increasing self-awareness is another benefit of having a healthy mind. When athletes are able to be more aware of their thoughts and emotions, they can better control them. This allows them to manage their stress levels and stay in the moment. As a result, they are able to perform at a higher level and achieve greater success.

On the field, court, ice, etc. being self-aware can allow you to control your actions and reactions during the game or during practice. If you know what is going on inside your head, then you can better control it. The ability to stay in the moment and allow all of the other things to fall away during a game is a powerful tool that all athletes can benefit from.

In one study, college football players who practiced mindfulness reported feeling less anxious and more relaxed during their games. They also had lower levels of cortisol, a hormone that is released in response to stress (Rooks, 2017).

The benefits of having a healthy mind are clear. For athletes, mindfulness can help to improve performance, lower stress levels, and increase self-awareness. If you're looking to improve your game, incorporating mindfulness into your training is a great place to start.

Increased Mental Toughness

Mental toughness is regarded as a key performance asset for athletes. It is understood by those in competitive sports as the ability to sustain attention on the task-at-hand while under pressure, as well as in the face of distraction (Jones et al. 2002). A number of studies have found that a healthy mind can help to increase mental toughness in athletes.

A study of collegiate rowers found that those who practiced mindfulness had increased levels of mental toughness (Kabat-Zinn, 2000). In the study, participants were given a four-week mindfulness training program. The results showed that the participants who received the mindfulness training had increased levels of mental toughness compared to those who did not receive the training. The same results were found with tennis players participating in a six-week mindfulness training program.

Tennis player Serena Williams is known for her focus and her ability to stay calm on the court.

"If you are behind in a game, it's so important to relax, and that's what I do -- when I'm behind in a game, that's when I become most relaxed. Just focus on one point at a time... just that sole point, and then the next one, and the next one," she has explained (Stillman, 2021).

Williams slows down her perception so she can "keep her eye on the ball," a technique that has led to her numerous wins. The only way to achieve this level of focus is through practice.

Improved Overall Health

Having a healthy mind isn't just about the way you think. It's also about the conscious choices you make daily such as eating well, getting enough sleep, and setting goals. All of these things contribute to your overall health and can have a positive impact on your performance.

When you're mindful of the choices you make, you're more likely to make ones that are good for you. You're also more likely to stick with them because you're aware of the benefits they provide. Making healthy choices becomes a habit, and that habit can lead to a healthier, happier, and more successful life.

The benefits of having a healthy mind are clear. For athletes, having a healthy mind can help to improve performance, lower stress levels, and increase self-awareness. If you're looking to improve your game, incorporating mindfulness into your training is a great place to start.

So, what are you waiting for?

Chapter 2: How to Win the Game in Your Head

How many times have you seen an athlete give up right before they make a comeback? How many times have you seen them choke under pressure? It's frustrating, isn't it? You know they have the talent, but they just can't seem to get it done. Well, the truth is, there is a mental side of sports that often can't overcome the physical side.

The mental side of sports is just as important as the physical side. In fact, it can often be the difference between winning and losing. The mental side of sports includes things like focus, concentration, motivation, and confidence. All of these factors can make a big difference in an athlete's performance.

The Mental Side of Sports

When it comes to sports, the physical side of the game is certainly important. After all, in order to win a match, you must have good technique and superior strength and agility. However, mental skills are also essential for success on the field, court, ice, or course. The ability to focus and be fully present in the moment allows you to perform at your best, even when you are pushed to the limit. Moreover, having a positive attitude and high self-confidence helps you to overcome obstacles and keep pushing forward, even in the face of adversity. The mental side of sports is crucial for achieving peak performance both on an individual level and as part of a team. When we truly believe in our abilities and take pride in our efforts, there is no limit to what we can accomplish on the field.

What are some of the benefits it can provide athletes?

Some benefits of improving the mental side of your game include improved focus, increased confidence, and the ability to cope with adversity better. When athletes are able to tap into their mental skills, they often find that they are able to perform at a higher level and achieve greater success. In addition, the mental side of sports can help athletes to better understand their opponents and what they are trying to accomplish. This can give you a major advantage on the field.

How can young athletes develop a strong mental game?

A strong mental game is essential for any young athlete who wants to reach their full potential. The ability to maintain focus, stay positive and manage emotions can be the difference between winning and losing.

There are a number of things that young athletes can do to develop a strong mental game.

First, it's important to set realistic goals and have a clear plan for reaching them.

Second, practice visualization techniques to help increase confidence and clarity on the playing field.

Third, focus on the present moment and don't dwell on past mistakes.

Finally, make sure to take care of your physical health by eating properly and getting enough rest.

This workbook will guide you through all of these topics to create a strong mental game and help you to become a better athlete and person.

What are some common obstacles athletes face when it comes to their mental health, and how can they overcome them?

When it comes to athletes and their mental health, there are a number of common obstacles that can get in the way. For example, many athletes may experience burnout or feelings of self-doubt when training for a big competition. Additionally, some athletes may struggle with the pressure of living up to their fans' expectations. Finally, many athletes may also have a hard time finding time for self-care or relaxation in the midst of their busy schedules.

There are a number of strategies that athletes can use to help overcome these obstacles. For one thing, they can work closely with a mental health professional who can provide them with the tools they need to manage stress and anxiety. In addition, they can take advantage of mindfulness practices like meditation or deep breathing exercises to stay centered and focused both in and out of competition. Ultimately, by taking proactive steps toward maintaining their well-being and reaching out for support when needed, athletes can succeed both on and off the field.

In this workbook, you will look at the specific obstacles you face and develop a plan to work through those obstacles.

What should athletes do if they feel like they're struggling with their mental health or if they know someone who is struggling?

If you are struggling with your mental health, it is important to reach out for help. There are a number of resources available to athletes who need support. For example, many sports teams have counselors or psychologists that athletes can talk to. In addition, there are hotlines like the National Suicide Prevention Lifeline (800-273-TALK). There is a resources section at the back of this workbook that includes numerous resources to help you if you are struggling.

How has the field of performance coaching evolved over the years, and where is it headed in the future?

The field of performance coaching has evolved considerably over the years, and it is continuing to evolve. In the past, performance coaches primarily focused on helping athletes overcome mental obstacles so that they could perform at their best. However, in recent years, there has been a shift toward a more holistic approach that takes into account the physical, mental, and emotional well-being of athletes. This shift is likely to continue in the future as more and more research is conducted on how to optimize athlete performance. Additionally, as mental health becomes less taboo, it is likely that even more athletes will seek out the help of performance coaches in order to improve their overall well-being.

This workbook focuses on that more holistic approach and looks at you, the athlete, as a whole person, not just a player on the field, a playmaker, or a winner. It will provide the tools and resources you need for life after sports.

Performance coaching myths debunked

One of the biggest myths about performance coaching is that it is only for elite or professional athletes. However, this could not be further from the truth! Performance coaching can be beneficial for athletes at all levels, from those just starting out to those who have been competing for many years.

Another myth is that performance coaches only work with athletes who are struggling. While it is true that performance coaches can help athletes overcome mental obstacles, they can also help athletes who are performing well to maintain their level of success.

So, whether you are still in high school, playing in college, an elite athlete or a weekend warrior, if you want to perform your best and improve your overall well-being, this workbook will be a valuable resource for you.

All Athletes Experience Mental Blocks

Any athlete will tell you that there are good days and bad days. On good days, everything comes together, and you feel like you can do anything. But on bad days, even the simplest task can seem impossible. This phenomenon is known as a mental block, and it can be incredibly frustrating. So why do mental blocks happen? There are actually a few different theories. Some experts believe that they're caused by anxiety or external pressure. Others believe that they're the result of negative thinking or past experiences. Whatever the cause, mental blocks can have a big impact on an athlete's performance. The good news is that there are a few things that can be done to overcome them. With some practice and effort, anyone can learn to silence their inner critic and focus on the task at hand.

What are the different types of mental blocks that athletes can experience?

There are actually a few different types of mental blocks that athletes can experience. One type is known as the "yips." The yips is a term used to describe when an athlete suddenly loses the ability to perform a task that they have previously been able to do with ease, for example, a pitcher who suddenly cannot throw strikes or a golfer who cannot make a putt. The yips can be caused by anxiety, external pressure, or negative thinking.

Another type of mental block is known as "choking." Choking occurs when an athlete performs poorly in a high-pressure situation. This can be due to nerves, overthinking, or trying to do too much. Choking is often the result of an athlete putting too much pressure on themselves to succeed.

The last type of mental block is known as "plateauing." Plateauing occurs when an athlete reaches a certain level of success and then has trouble progressing further. This can be due to a lack of motivation, overconfidence, or simply becoming too comfortable. Plateauing is often the result of an athlete not pushing themselves to reach their full potential.

While all three of these types of mental blocks can be frustrating, there are a few things that can be done to overcome them. With some practice and effort, anyone can learn to silence their inner critic and focus on the task

How do you know if you're experiencing a mental block?

There are a few different ways to tell if you're experiencing a mental block. One way is to pay attention to your thoughts. If you find yourself constantly doubting yourself or thinking negative thoughts, it's likely that you're experiencing a mental block. Another way to tell is to pay attention to your emotions. If you're feeling anxious or stressed, it's also likely that you're experiencing a mental block. The last way to tell is to pay attention to your performance. If you find yourself performing below your usual standards, it's likely that you're experiencing a mental block.

What should you do if you think you're experiencing a mental block?

If you think you're experiencing a mental block, the first thing you should do is take a step back and assess the situation. Try to identify what is causing your mental block. Once you've identified the cause, it will be easier to find a way to overcome it.

There are a few different ways to overcome a mental block. One way is to practice visualization. This involves picturing yourself succeeding in your mind. Another way is to use positive self-talk. This involves talking to yourself in a positive way and repeating affirmations. The last way is to take deep breaths and focus on the present moment. This will help you to calm your nerves and focus on the task at hand.

These techniques will be covered in-depth with practice exercises in this workbook.

How can athletes prevent themselves from experiencing mental blocks in the first place?

Practicing mindfulness and having a plan in place when obstacles do arise are both key ways to prevent mental blocks from occurring in the first place.

This workbook will teach you mindfulness techniques and guide you through the process of creating your plan to develop a healthy mindset.

What are the consequences of not dealing with a mental block?

If a mental block is not dealt with, it can lead to long-term consequences such as a loss of confidence, decreased motivation, and even depression. It can lead to poor performance in practice, during games, at school, at home, and at work. It can also lead to social withdrawal and a feeling of isolation.

It is important to deal with mental blocks as soon as they arise in order to prevent these long-term consequences.

This workbook will provide you with the tools you need to deal with mental blocks and get back on track to achieving your goals.

Chapter 3: The Assessment

In order to figure out how to move forward, it is necessary to take a look at your current situation to find out what is working and what isn't. By breaking down your life into smaller, manageable pieces, it's much easier to see where you succeed and what is holding you back.

In his book *Essentialism*, Greg McKeown wrote, "Essentialism is not about how to get more things done; it's about how to get the right things done... It is about making the wisest possible investment of your time and energy in order to operate at our highest point of contribution by doing only what is essential (McKeown, 2022)".

By focusing on what is essential and eliminating the things that don't serve you, it becomes much easier to set achievable goals, create systems that work, and find success to keep you motivated.

As you work through the questions in this chapter, take time to reflect on each of your answers before moving forward. At the end of the assessment, you will have all of the pieces needed to move through the rest of the workbook as you create a healthy mindset and a system that serves you in focusing your time and energy on accomplishing your goals.

Reflect and Celebrate

List three things you are currently thankful for.

1.

2.

3.

List three things you have accomplished that you are proud of.

1.

2.

3.

List three things that you have overcome in the past.

1.

2.

3.

What lessons did you learn about yourself through achieving those accomplishments and overcoming challenges?

What lessons did you learn about others as you worked to achieve those accomplishments overcoming challenges?

Part of having a healthy mindset is not only thinking about actions but thinking about your thoughts and feelings.

How did you feel when you reached those accomplishments?

How did you feel when facing obstacles and challenges?

Did you allow yourself to experience those feelings? Why or why not?

Which of those feelings do you want to hold onto, and which do you want to let go of?

Set Intentions

Think of three words that can be your guideposts as you move forward. Some examples that people have used in the past include healthy, intentional, confident, peaceful, bold, compassionate, and strong.

Reframe and Master Mindsets

In order to change your mindset to a healthy mindset, you must first identify what your current mindsets are.

There are two types of mindsets: fixed mindsets and growth mindsets. People with fixed mindsets believe that their talents and abilities are set in stone, whereas people with growth mindsets believe that they can develop their talents and abilities through hard work, good teaching, and persistence (Dweck, 2022).

Which mindset do you have?

Fixed mindset: I have a certain amount of talent and ability, and I can't really do much to change it.

Growth mindset: I can develop my talents and abilities through hard work, good teaching, and persistence.

Which of the following best describes your current situation?

I am in a rut, and I don't see a way out.

I have some goals that I would like to achieve, but I'm not sure how to go about them.

I am pretty happy with where I am in life, but there are always areas that could use improvement.

If you are in a rut and don't see a way out, it is essential to take a look at your current situation to find out what is working and what isn't. Once you have a better understanding of your current situation, you can begin to set goals and create a plan to achieve them.

It is possible to have a fixed mindset in some areas of life and a growth mindset in others. Let's take a look at what your mindsets currently are.

Here are some examples of fixed mindsets:

When facing	My inner voice says...
Challenges	There is no way I can do that.
Failures	I stink at sports.

Conflicts	*I'm just a terrible person.*
Criticism	*I'll never be good enough.*
Mistakes	*I can't do anything right.*

Take some time to think about your mindsets for each situation.

When facing	My inner voice says…
Challenges	
Failures	
Conflicts	
Criticism	
Mistakes	

You have a choice with what your inner voice says. As you look at your answers, are you happy with the way you talk to yourself? Is the way you talk to yourself healthy? Would you talk to someone else that way?

It is possible to shift your mindset. It just takes training. It's no different than drills in practice; only you are focusing on the mental instead of the physical.

Let's take those fixed mindsets and change them to growth mindsets.

Look back at your answers above and think about how you can reframe each mindset. Here is an example.

When facing	*I can reframe my mindset to say*
Challenges	*I can learn to do that. Go for it. Make it happen!*
Failures	*Everyone fails. Time spent learning is never wasted time. How can I approach this from a different angle?*

Conflicts	*I don't always need to be right or included. Disagreements will happen, and that doesn't mean I am unloved or unwanted. I can listen and communicate better.*
Criticism	*I am good enough, but there is always room for improvement.*
Mistakes	*You can't grow without trying new things, and it's ok to mess up. What can I learn, and who can I ask for help?*

Now it's your turn. Take your mindsets from above, which are fixed mindsets and think about how you can change those mindsets to growth mindsets.

When facing	My inner voice says…
Challenges	
Failures	
Conflicts	
Criticism	
Mistakes	

Trying to tackle all of your fixed mindsets at one time will not serve you well. You will be trying to tackle too many challenges at once, so pick the one mindset you want to start working on and write it here.

_____

What actionable steps can you take to start changing your mindset? For example, if you've chosen to work on your mindset when faced with challenges, you may decide to stop, realize that you can do it, and break the challenge into smaller steps.

Identify and Prioritize Your Values

The next step is to identify and prioritize your values. Some examples of values include family, relationships, personal growth, health, spirituality, creativity, mental health, loyalty, honesty, toughness, determination, courage, and generosity.

List up to five values that are important to you.

1.

2.

3.

4.

5.

Now let's rank those values in order of importance and reflect on how you currently act on those values.

My Values	
Health	*I've been consistent with workouts, but I don't make healthy food choices.*
1.	
2.	

3.	
4.	
5.	

Now take some time to set some intentions to prioritize those values going forward.

My Values	
Health	*I need to prepare healthy snacks ahead of time so they are as easy to grab as unhealthy choices.*
1.	
2.	
3.	
4.	
5.	

You may want to bookmark this assessment section, as we will refer back to it throughout the rest of the workbook.

Being an athlete requires more than just physical training - it's important to have a healthy mindset as well. That's why I'm excited to offer my Healthy Mindset for Athletes 30-Day Program. With this program, you'll receive targeted assessment, coaching, and motivation to help you reach your full potential. You'll also have access to the app for ongoing accountability. So, if you're ready to take your game to the next level, sign up today and let's get started! Use the code COUPON1 to receive a 50% discount.

Chapter 4: Setting Goals

Do you want to be a better athlete, student, person, or employee? Of course, you do! Nobody enjoys being bad at something. In order to improve, you need to set goals and work towards them.

What is a goal?

For athletes, setting and achieving goals is a key part of becoming successful. A goal is a specific target that an athlete sets for themselves, with the intention of reaching it. Goals can be related to any aspect of an athlete's performance, from improving their personal best to winning a championship.

Athletes often set both short-term, medium, and long-term goals, in order to keep themselves motivated and on track. Achieving goals can give athletes a sense of accomplishment and pride, as well as help them to build confidence and improve their overall performance. While setting goals can be challenging, it is important for athletes to remember that even small improvements can make a big difference in their success.

What is a short-term goal?

A short-term goal is something that an athlete sets to accomplish in a relatively short time frame, typically within one to three weeks. These goals can vary in nature, ranging from increasing endurance or speed to improving particular skills or techniques. For example, a runner might focus on increasing her pace during sprints or building up her lung capacity through regular cardio workouts.

Regardless of the focus, short-term goals are designed to help athletes gain skills and achieve performance goals more quickly and effectively. Whether you're an athlete or simply someone who wants to reach your fitness goals more quickly, setting short-term goals can be an effective way to stay motivated and focused on your ultimate objectives.

Some specific examples of short-term hockey goals could include:

- Shooting for a higher percentage on net during practice

- Working on developing a more accurate wrist shot

- Increasing speed and agility in short bursts

- Practicing puck control in tight areas

- Doing explosive exercises that improve skating

What is a medium-term goal?

A medium-term goal generally takes between four and twelve weeks to achieve, such as in a single season. For example, a runner who is training for a 5K race might set a medium-term goal of running four days per week and increasing their mileage by 10% each week. By setting and achieving small goals like this on a regular basis, athletes can make steady progress towards their long-term goals. Medium-term goals can help keep athletes motivated and focused on their training, preventing them from becoming discouraged or burned out.

When setting medium-term goals, it is important to strike a balance between challenging oneself and remaining realistic; if a goal is too easy, it won't be effective in helping the athlete improve, but if it is too difficult, it may lead to frustration. Ultimately, the best way to find the right balance is to experiment and see what works best for the individual athlete.

Some specific examples of medium-term soccer goals could include:

- Improving ball control in tight areas

- Working on developing a stronger shot

- Becoming more proficient at heading the ball

- Increasing speed and agility over short distances

- Conditioning your body to be able to play for an extended period of time without becoming fatigued

What is a long-term goal?

A long-term goal is something that you work towards gradually over a period of time, with the ultimate aim of achieving success in a particular field. For athletes, this might mean working towards winning an Olympic gold medal or setting a new world record in their given sport. Whether your goal is athletic or not, though, it should be something that invigorates and inspires you, fueling your drive to succeed no matter what challenges you may face along the way.

If you are looking for an outlet to direct your ambition and determination, remember that a long-term goal can provide the motivation and focus needed to reach your full potential and achieve great things. Just remember to stay dedicated, keep pushing yourself, and dream big!

Some specific examples of long-term football goals could include:

- Becoming a more complete player by working on your strengths and weaknesses

- Improving your stamina so that you can last the entire game without becoming fatigued

- Training to become faster and more agile so you can make defensive plays more easily

- Developing better ball control so that you can keep possession more effectively

- Playing ball in college or the NFL

How do I start setting goals?

As an athlete, it is important to set goals in order to improve your performance and achieve success. But how do you go about setting goals?

First, you need to identify what you want to achieve. Are you looking to run a personal best in the marathon? Win a gold medal at the Olympics? Once you have a goal in mind, you need to develop a plan of action. What steps do you need to take in order to reach your goal? For example, if you are looking to improve your marathon time, you may need to train more frequently or change your diet. Once you have a plan of action, it is important to stay motivated and focused on your goal. Remember, setting goals is the first step on the road to success!

The SMART Method

One of the best ways to set goals is by using the SMART method. This means that your goals should be Specific, Measurable, Achievable, Realistic, and Time-Based. Let's break this down a bit further.

Your goal should be specific. This means that you need to know exactly what it is that you want to achieve. For example, rather than setting a goal to "run faster," you should set a goal to "improve my marathon time by two minutes."

Your goal should be measurable. This means that you need to have a way of tracking your progress and determining whether or not you are actually achieving your goal. In the example above, you could measure your progress by timing yourself during training runs and races.

Your goal should be achievable. This means that your goal should be something that is actually within the realm of possibility. If you are a beginner runner, setting a goal to run a four-minute mile is probably not realistic. However, setting a goal to improve your marathon time by two minutes is definitely achievable!

Your goal should be realistic. This means that your goal should be something that you can actually achieve, given the resources and time available to you. For example, if you only have four weeks to train for a marathon, setting a goal to run a personal best is probably not realistic. However, setting a goal to improve your marathon time by two minutes is definitely realistic!

Your goal should be time-based. This means that you need to set a deadline for yourself in order to stay on track. In the example above, you could set a goal to improve your marathon time by two minutes in four weeks. This would give you a specific timeline to work with and help you stay motivated.

Now that you know how to set goals using the SMART method, it's time to put this knowledge into action!

Envision the Future

Setting goals requires envisioning your future life and where you want to go. This means having a clear and concise vision of what you want to achieve. For example, if your goal is to run a personal best in the marathon, you need to visualize yourself crossing the finish line with a time that is two minutes faster than your current personal record. What does this look like? How does it feel? By envisioning your future success, you can stay motivated and focused on your goal.

Take some time to answer the following questions before moving forward. Your long-term goals do not have to be related to your sport only. They could be related to personal or career goals as well.

Where do I see myself in one year?

Where do I see myself in three years?

Where do I see myself in five years?

Where do I see myself in ten years?

What is your biggest dream?

Let's begin making your long-term goals SMART.

What do I need to accomplish in order to be where I want to be? Remember, long-term goals take time to accomplish.

List your long-term goals in the chart below and check whether each goal is SMART.

Goal	Specific	Measurable	Attainable	Realistic	Time-based
Help my team make it to the state championship game my senior year	√	√	√	√	√

Now let's take those long-term goals and break them down into medium-term goals. Medium-term goals generally take between four to twelve weeks.

Goal	Specific	Measurable	Attainable	Realistic	Time-based
Increase my goal scoring by 20%	√	√	√	√	√

What steps can you take daily as your short-term goals to help achieve those medium and long-term goals?

Goal	Specific	Measurable	Attainable	Realistic	Time-based
Practice scoring drills daily	√	√	√	√	√

Staying Motivated to Achieve Your Goals

One of the most difficult things about setting and achieving goals is staying motivated. It is easy to get discouraged when you don't see results right away or if you have a setback. However, it is important to remember that progress takes time. Trust the process and be patient!

Todd Elik was never supposed to make it. The NHL draft came and went without his name being called. He was passed over by every team multiple times. But instead of letting that discourage him, Todd used it as motivation. He worked harder than ever before and eventually made it to the NHL.

Elik was always a gifted player, but he really came into his own after joining the Rangers organization. His 100-point season in the IHL showed everyone that he had the potential to be a top scorer at the NHL level, and he didn't disappoint. Elik may not have been the biggest or most talented player, but he always gave 110% and left everything on the ice (*Todd Elik*, n.d.).

Your motivation should come from within and not from what people say about you. If you allow others to dictate how you feel, you will never reach your potential. Surround yourself with positive people who support your dreams and goals. These are the people who will help push you to achieve greatness!

What keeps you motivated?

It is important to have an answer to this question because motivation ebbs and flows. There will be days when you don't feel like working towards your goals, and that is okay! On these days, it is important to think about what keeps you going.

What keeps me going?

Celebrate Accomplishments Along the Way

One of the best ways to stay motivated is to celebrate your accomplishments along the way. Acknowledge how far you have come, and be proud of your progress! This will help keep you going when times are tough.

What are some recent accomplishments I can celebrate?

Chapter 5: Creating Systems that Work

Manon Rheaume was the first woman to play in an American men's sports league. She signed a contract with the Tampa Bay Lightning in 1992 and played in exhibition games until signing her first professional contract that same year with IHL team, the Atlanta Knights. Rheaume had a huge dream to accomplish something no woman had ever accomplished before. But she had a plan to get there (Manon Rhéaume – the First Woman to Play in an American Men's pro Sports League, 2021).

Rheaume said, "If you persevere long enough, if you do the right things long enough, the right things will happen."

Do you ever feel like you're just spinning your wheels? That no matter how hard you work, you can't seem to get ahead? You're not alone. Many athletes feel this way. The way to achieve goals is by creating systems that work. The good news is that there are specific steps you can take to create those systems.

In Atomic Habits, James Clear writes, "You do not rise to the level of your goals. You fall to the level of your systems. Your goal is your desired outcome. Your system is the collection of daily habits that will get you there" (Clear, 2018).

Before you start setting goals, it's important to take a look at your current systems and how they work for you or if they fail you.

Create Daily Habits and Rituals

Daily habits are important because they are the building blocks of your system. They are the things you do every day that will help you reach your goals. If your habits are inconsistent or if they don't align with your goals and values, you will not be able to achieve success.

Let's start by looking at your daily habits. Fill out the chart below with what a typical day looks like for you.

Time of day	Typical activities
Morning	
Afternoon	
Evening	

Take a look back at the self-assessment and copy your values here.

1.

2.

3.

4.

5.

Now take a look back at your short-term goals from Chapter 4 and copy them here.

What responsibilities do you have each day?

Do your daily habits reflect your goals, values, and responsibilities? If not, it's time to establish a better daily routine.

A habit is a routine or behavior that you perform regularly. It can be something as simple as brushing your teeth every day or as complex as maintaining your responsibilities at school, home, and work.

Creating a daily routine can help you become more productive, efficient, and effective. It can also help reduce stress and anxiety. But most importantly, it can help you achieve your goals and maintain a healthy mindset.

Establish a Daily Routine

A good morning routine helps you get the day started off on the right foot. It sets the tone for the day and gets you in the right mindset to achieve your goals. However, a good morning routine doesn't start in the morning. It starts the night before.

An evening routine is just as important as a morning routine. It helps you wind down from the day and prepare for a good night's sleep. This is important because quality sleep is essential for optimal performance. We will cover more about sleep in a later chapter.

Creating an evening routine starts with setting a bedtime. This is the time you plan to be in bed and asleep. Your bedtime should be based on the time you need to wake up. If you need to wake up at 6 am, your bedtime should be around eight hours before, so 10 pm. Once you have a bedtime, start working backward to create your evening routine.

For example, if your bedtime is 10 pm, you may want to start getting ready for bed at 9 pm. This gives you time to brush your teeth, wash your face, and take care of any nighttime responsibilities.

This is also a good time to consider any nighttime rituals that will help you relax and wind down, such as visualizing your goals, meditating, reading, or listening to music.

After you have a general idea of your evening routine, it's time to start filling in the details.

Bedtime:

Responsibilities:

Habits:

Rituals:

Let's start planning your morning routine. Your morning should include three main components: physical activity, breakfast, and your daily goal setting.

Your physical activity can be anything from a walk around the block to a full workout at the gym. It doesn't matter what you do as long as you get your body moving.

Breakfast is important because it breaks the overnight fast and gives you energy for the day. It doesn't have to be a big meal, but it should be something that will give you sustained energy. We will talk more about fueling your body through nutrition in a later chapter.

Your goal setting should include writing down your top priority for the day and creating a plan of action to achieve it. This is important because it helps you stay focused on your goals and values.

Physical Activity:

Daily Goals:

Now that you have a plan to start and end each day, you can start planning your day to achieve your goals. Start by looking at your daily schedule and identify any free time you have. This is time that you can use to establish new habits or rituals through your short-term goals. Then, decide what activities you will do during this time.

You don't form new habits overnight. It takes time, effort, and consistency. But if you stick with it, eventually, it will become a part of your daily routine. And before you know it, you will be one step closer to achieving your goals.

Remember, your goal is to establish a daily routine that reflects your goals, values, and responsibilities. So, take some time to plan your days, weeks, and months accordingly. And don't forget to have some fun along the way!

Don't forget that your systems are always in motion. They will need to be adjusted as your life changes. The goal is to find a system that works for you and stick with it, then adjust as needed.

Chapter 6: Developing a Positive Self-Image

Michael Phelps is one of the most decorated Olympians of all time. In his career, he amassed an incredible twenty-eight medals, with twenty-three of those being gold. He set both all-time Olympic records. Phelps did so over the course of four Olympic games spanning twelve years. Phelps also overcame a lot of self-doubt along the way.

When Phelps was younger, he was diagnosed with ADHD and told by his doctor that he would never amount to anything. Phelps's mom used this as motivation for him to succeed. Phelps's first coach didn't think he was good enough to make the Olympic team. This only made Phelps work harder, and he went on to prove his coach wrong by not only making the team but becoming one of the most decorated Olympians of all time (Valentine, 2019).

Phelps said, "You dream. You plan. You reach. There will be obstacles. There will be doubters. There will be mistakes. But with hard work, with belief, with confidence and trust in yourself and those around you, there are no limits."

All of the best-laid plans and systems will not serve you if you do not believe in your ability to accomplish your goals.

Look back at the self-assessment from chapter 3. Do you regularly talk to yourself in a negative manner or a positive one?

Everyone struggles with self-image, including Michael Phelps. No one is perfect, and everyone has their own insecurities. Phelps was able to overcome his doubts and achieve great things because he had a positive self-image. He believed in himself and his abilities, even when others did not.

If you struggle with self-image, there are things you can do to improve it.

Talk to yourself in a positive manner. It can be difficult to have a positive self-image, but it is important. When you talk to yourself in a positive manner, you are more likely to believe in yourself and your abilities. You are also more likely to take action and achieve your goals.

Focus on your positive qualities and what you have accomplished rather than your negative qualities or what you have not accomplished. It is important to be realistic, but it is also important to focus on the positive.

Be accepting of yourself. You are not perfect, and you never will be. Accepting yourself for who you are is an important part of having a positive self-image.

Set realistic goals. If you set goals that are too high, you are setting yourself up for disappointment. Set goals that are realistic and achievable.

Work on your self-image every day. Just like anything else, it takes time and effort to improve your self-image. Work on it every day, even if it is just a little bit.

Surround yourself with positive people. Being around positive people can help you to see the good in yourself.

Avoid comparisons. Comparing yourself to others is a surefire way to feel bad about yourself. Everyone is different and has their own unique qualities.

Focus on your journey, not the destination. The destination is important, but it is not the only thing that matters. Focus on your journey and enjoy the process.

Forgive your mistakes. We all make mistakes. What matters is how we learn from our mistakes and move on.

Practice gratitude. Be thankful for what you have and where you are on your journey.

Appreciate your accomplishments. Take the time to celebrate your accomplishments, no matter how small.

Stay positive when things get tough. Things will not always go your way. When things get tough, stay positive and trust in yourself.

Be patient - change doesn't happen overnight. It takes time to develop a positive self-image. Be patient and trust in the process.

Chapter 7: Maintaining Confidence in Yourself

It's easy to lose confidence in yourself. We all have off days and bad moments where we don't feel our best. But it's important to remember that these moments are just a part of life, and they don't define who you are as a person or as an athlete. It's also important to remember that your confidence is something that you have to work on every day.

When it comes to winning, Mark Messier knows a thing or two. A six-time Stanley Cup champion, Messier is the second most prolific playoff points scorer of all time. He's also a two-time most valuable player in the NHL, a 15-time all-star, and the only person ever to captain two different teams to Stanley Cup championships—the Edmonton Oilers (even after the departure of his great friend Wayne Gretzky) and the New York Rangers. Simply put, Messier is a winner. But he's also so much more than that. He's a leader, motivator, and an inspiration to everyone who has ever had the privilege of playing with him or watching him play. He's the epitome of class, competitiveness, and character. In other words, he's everything you want in a hockey player—and more. So, it's no wonder that, when it comes to winning, Mark Messier is always at the top of his game.

But even players as prolific as Messier struggle with confidence. Everyone struggles with developing and maintaining confidence.

"Even at the peak of my career, I would struggle at times. I was fortunate enough that we had sports psychology seminars at a very early age, basically the first year of my career when I was 18 years old. I kept it with me my whole career," Messier said in an interview. "Self-confidence is huge, and a big part of that is self-talk—when things aren't going well, not to be negative. You have to figure out what went wrong, so you're able to move on from any failure" (Smith, 2022).

What causes you to lose confidence in yourself?

Confidence Comes from Within

Confidence comes from within. It is a state of mind that allows you to trust yourself and your abilities. When you are confident, you feel good about yourself and your abilities, and this inner feeling shows through in your interactions with others.

Maintaining confidence can be challenging, especially when things don't go your way. However, it is important to remember that everyone experiences setbacks and failures. What matters is how you respond to them.

Here are some ways to maintain confidence in yourself:

Believe in yourself. This may sound like common sense, but it's important to remind yourself that you are capable and competent. When you catch yourself doubting your abilities, reframe your thinking and remind yourself of your past successes.

Be prepared. One way to build confidence is to be prepared for whatever situation you find yourself in. If you know what to expect and are ready for it, you will feel more confident and less likely to be thrown off by unexpected challenges.

Practice. Another way to build confidence is to practice. If you can master a skill or task through repetition, you will feel more confident when it comes time to use that skill or perform that task in a real-world setting.

Be positive. Confidence is also linked to your outlook on life. If you focus on the negative, you will tend to see yourself in a negative light. However, if you focus on the positive, you will be more likely to see yourself in a positive light.

Keep learning. Finally, one of the best ways to maintain confidence is to keep learning. When you are constantly learning and expanding your knowledge base, you will feel more confident in your abilities.

Maintaining confidence is something that you have to work on every day. It doesn't come naturally to everyone, and even the most successful people have to work at it.

In the face of defeat, maintain confidence and persevere. This is a quality that all great athletes possess. When they lose, they don't let it get them down. They use it as motivation to come back stronger the next time.

Michael Jordan said, "I've missed more than 9,000 shots in my career. I've lost almost 300 games. Twenty-six times I've been trusted to take the game-winning shot and missed. I've failed over and over and over again in my life. And that is why I succeed."

The same goes for life in general. When you're facing tough times, maintain confidence in yourself and don't give up.

Remember, success is the sum of small efforts repeated day in and day out. So, keep at it and don't give up! Confidence is the key to success.

Look back at the mindsets you want to work on from the self-assessment. List any negative self-talk that causes you to doubt yourself.

What steps listed above can you take to improve your self-confidence, and how can you incorporate those into your daily habits and rituals?

Overcome Adversity

Any difficult situation or event that causes emotional pain or difficulty. Adversity can come in many different forms, such as personal loss, illness, or financial hardship. It can be tough to get through tough times, but it is important to remember that you are not alone. Many people have faced and overcome adversity.

Lean on your support system. When you're going through tough times, it's important to lean on your support system. This can include family, friends, or a professional counselor. These people can offer you love, comfort, and practical help when you need it most.

Messier said, "Everybody needs help no matter what position you're in, no matter where you are in your own life. The biggest thing that has come out of all of this is that there's no shame in admitting any problem, and seeking help has been very productive and helpful for a lot of folks" (Smith, 2022).

Keep things in perspective. It is also important to keep things in perspective. While it may feel like the end of the world, it is important to remember that there are people who have it worse off than you. This doesn't minimize your pain, but it can help you put things into perspective and give you some perspective.

Find a positive outlet. Finally, one of the best ways to deal with adversity is to find a positive outlet. This can be anything from writing in a journal to taking up a new hobby to giving your all on the field. Doing something that makes you happy can help you get through tough times.

No one is immune to adversity, but how you deal with it is what matters most.

What types of adversity are you facing right now?

How does that make you feel?

When you're going through a tough time, it's important to accept how you feel. Don't try to bottle your emotions up because that will only make things worse. Accept that you are feeling pain, sadness, or anger and allow yourself to feel those emotions.

It's also important to remember that you are not alone. Many people have faced and overcome adversity. There is no shame in admitting that you need help, and seeking help can be very productive. If you need immediate help, there are resources available at the end of this book.

Embrace the feeling of adversity. It can be tough, but it is also a sign that you are alive. Feeling pain means that you care about something and that you are invested in your life. Don't try to numb yourself to the feeling of adversity. Instead, embrace it and use it as motivation to become stronger.

Use the feeling of adversity to your advantage. It can be a powerful motivator to push yourself harder and achieve your goals. Let it motivate you to become the best version of yourself.

How can you channel your feelings into motivation to achieve your goals?

What lessons can you take from your experiences? How can you use those lessons to become a better person?

Chapter 8: Building Your Teamwork Skills

Do you ever feel like your team could be working a little better together? If so, you're not alone. A lot of teams struggle to communicate and collaborate effectively. This can lead to frustration and conflict. Fortunately, there is a way to build teamwork skills that is both mindful and effective: through sports!

Being A Team Player Starts with You

Being a team player is all about working together to achieve a common goal. It's not about putting your own needs ahead of the team's or trying to be the star of the show. In fact, doing so can actually be detrimental to the team's success. Teamwork is about supporting your teammates and working together to get the job done. In fact, putting your own needs ahead of the team's can actually be detrimental to the team's success. When everyone is working together and on the same page, that's when teams are at their best. So next time you're feeling tempted to put your own needs ahead of the team's, remember that being a team player means putting the team first.

Being a team player has its benefits. When you work together with a group towards a common goal, you can get more done than working alone. You can communicate better and learn how to work better as a team. These skills are essential in many workplaces and can give you an advantage in your career. Being a team player can also help you stay fit and healthy. Research has shown that people who exercise with a partner or in a group are more likely to stick with their workout routine than those who go it alone. Whether you're playing on a sports team or working on a project at work, being a team player is good for you.

In order to be a successful team player, there are a few things you need to do. First, it's important that you be supportive of your teammates. This means encouraging them and helping them out when they need it. Second, communication is key. You need to make sure you are clear about what you need and what you expect from your teammates. Lastly, you need to work together to achieve the team's goals. Remember, it's not about you; it's about the team!

When I was playing in the NHL, I had a teammate who went above and beyond to help me out. He faked an injury when we were playing for the Buffalo Sabres. I needed to play 70 Games for a bonus and a one-way contract. He and seven other players went to management the morning of the game to reassure me that I would be in the lineup. It worked out as Mark, and the other players went to bat for me.

Despite the help from my teammates, it looked like I would not get my 70th game that season. That's when Mark Napier and Larry Playfair, two of the best men I've ever met, stepped in. Mark Napier was in the last year of his 17-year career. He was a player who had been on two Stanley Cup-winning teams and was an amazing player and an amazing man. Larry Playfair stood up to the general manager and said he would not play and that I should be put on in his place. Unfortunately, Larry was a defenseman, and I was a forward, so his plan needed a bit of help from Mark Napier.

During warm-ups before the last game of the season, Mark Napier nodded at me and then winked. He then grabbed his leg, shouting about the pain. Yes, he faked an injury with one clear intention. I was there, warming up, and I played Mark's position. With him out, I would have to go into the game.

Mark Napier is known for his offensive talents on the ice. However, he was also one of the best teammates anyone could ask for. He supported the other players, was a great leader, and gave me the best gift any player can give another. Napier faked an injury to help ensure I got a one-way contract and bonus.

I'm not saying you need to put it all on the line like Napier did for me, but showing respect, compassion, and support for every one of your teammates is incredibly important. There isn't really a team at all without those vital elements.

Think about the way you treat and interact with your teammates. What areas do you need to work on?

Is there anyone that you need to treat with more respect, compassion and support?

[ ]

What actionable steps will you take to improve your effectiveness as a teammate?

[ ]

Communication is Critical

In order to be a successful team player, communication is key. You need to be clear about what you need and what you expect from your teammates. This includes making sure everyone is on the same page and knows what the goal is. If everyone isn't working towards the same objective, it'll be difficult to achieve anything. Good communication also means being able to listen to others and understand their perspective. It's important to be able to see where they're coming from so that you can find common ground. Lastly, don't forget to stay positive and encourage your teammates. A little motivation can go a long way in helping everyone give their best effort.

Communication is also important for problem-solving. If there are any issues or conflicts, it's important to be able to talk through them and come up with a solution that everyone can agree on. This can be difficult, but it's important to remember that you're all working towards the same goal. It's also important to be respectful of everyone's opinions and ideas. Just because you don't agree with someone doesn't mean their idea is bad.

How can I improve my communication with my team?

What are some things I can do to encourage and motivate my teammates?

What is one thing I can do to be more respectful of others' opinions and ideas?

In order to be a successful team player, you need to work together with your teammates to achieve the team's goals. This means being willing to put the team's needs first and working together to find solutions. It can be difficult to do this, but it's important to remember that you're all working towards the same goal.

Mindfulness is an Important Teamwork Skill

Since mindfulness is the practice of being present and aware, it can help you to be more aware of your thoughts, feelings, and actions. This can lead to better communication and collaboration with others. It can lead to better performance in sports, as well.

Why is having a healthy mindset important for teams?

A healthy mindset is essential for success in any endeavor. When you have a healthy mindset, you're more likely to see the positive in situations. This can help you to be more resilient when things don't go as planned. It can also help you to be more supportive of your teammates. A healthy mindset is also essential for maintaining a healthy lifestyle. When you have a healthy mindset, you're more likely to make healthy choices. You're also more likely to stick to your goals. A healthy mindset is the foundation for a healthy life.

A healthy mindset is also essential for any athletic team. Though you start with a positive attitude and a belief in yourself, that attitude needs to extend toward your teammates as well. It includes setting goals together and working hard to achieve them. It involves staying focused and disciplined, even when things are tough. And it requires a willingness to learn from mistakes and keep moving forward. A team with a healthy mindset is one that is mentally tough and prepared to face whatever challenges come its way. Such a team is poised for success both on and off the playing field.

Being a good teammate means more than just showing up to games. It means being there for your teammates, day in and day out. It means working hard in practice, even when you're not feeling your best. It means being a supportive friend, both on and off the field. Good teammates are the glue that holds a team together. They're the ones who lift their teammates up when they're down and who push them to be their best. If you want to be a good teammate, start by showing up and giving it you're all in practice. The rest will follow.

In 2010, the 4-man bobsled team from the US was trying to do something that hadn't been achieved in 62 years, win Olympic Gold. Steve Melser led his team (Curtis Tomasevicz, Steve Holcomb, and Justin Olsen) through insurmountable odds and a difficult track to win gold.

"We train countless hours to perform at the highest level in the world for five seconds at a time," Mesler said. "If all four of us aren't in the same mindset to ensure that that time spent is as close to perfect as we can be, then it's all for naught. Coming together in intense moments to perform as a team is the essence of Olympic bobsled (Radvillas, 2020)".

56

Healthy Mindset Skills for Teams

Here are some mindful teamwork skills for athletes:

Be present: Pay attention to what is happening in the here and now. This includes your own thoughts and feelings, as well as the thoughts and feelings of others.

Be aware of your body: Notice how your body feels when you are playing. This can help you to be more aware of your own physical state and the physical state of others.

Be aware of your breath: Taking deep breaths can help you to relax and focus. This can also help you to be more aware of your own emotions and the emotions of others.

Be kind: Treat yourself and others with kindness and respect. This includes speaking kindly, listening mindfully, and being considerate of others' needs.

Visualize: Use your imagination to visualize yourself and others succeeding. This can help you to focus and stay positive.

Set an intention: Before you start practicing or playing, take a moment to set an intention. This can help you to focus on what is important to you and your team.

What are some other mindful teamwork skills that your team practices?

What are some healthy mindsets that your team needs?

Mindfulness has been used successfully in sports teams in a variety of ways. Some teams use mindfulness to help them stay focused and disciplined. Others use it to build rapport and trust among teammates. And still, others use it to deal with stress and adversity.

How can you incorporate a healthy mindset with your team?

- Talk to your coach about incorporating some of these mindful teamwork skills into your practice.

- Do some research on mindfulness and sports teams. There are many books and articles that you can read to learn more about how to use mindfulness with your team.

The most important thing is to get started and see how mindfulness can help your team. There is no one right way to use mindfulness, so experiment and find what works best for you and your teammates.

Chapter 9: Handling Pressure and Criticism Effectively

As an athlete, you will inevitably face criticism and pressure at some point in your career. You will inevitably make mistakes. It is how you handle these situations that will determine your success. Some athletes crumble under pressure, while others thrive. The key to handling criticism and pressure lies in having a healthy mindset.

Look back at the assessment from Chapter 3.

Did you have a fixed or a growth mindset when it comes to criticism and mistakes?

```

```

What type of negative self-talk did you have about criticism and mistakes?

```

```

How did you decide to reframe those mindsets?

```

```

You Are Not Your Mistakes or Failures

You're not your mistakes or your failures. You're not the time you wasted or the opportunities you missed. You're not the bad decisions you made or the person you used to be. You're not your regrets or your shame. You're not your past. You are so much more than that. You are the lessons you learned from your mistakes. You are the wisdom you gained from your experiences. You are the strength you built up from overcoming difficult times. You are the person you've become because of everything you've been through. And you are so much more than just your mistakes. So don't let them define you or hold you back.

As any athlete knows, mistakes are a part of the game. Whether it's a missed shot or a dropped pass, everyone makes them. The important thing is to learn from your mistakes and not let them get you down. After all, a mistake is just an action, not a personality or a person.

What was the last mistake you made?

How did you react?

So how can you react better to your mistakes? The key is to have a healthy mindset. Instead of berating yourself for every little thing, try to be more understanding and forgiving. Accept that everyone makes mistakes, and that's okay. Remind yourself that making mistakes is a natural part of the learning process. And most importantly, don't give up. Instead, use your mistakes as motivation to keep going and do better next time.

A study published in the National Library of Medicine shows that Olympic gold medalists considered setbacks essential to their eventual wins (Sarkar et al., 2015).

A healthy mindset is key, especially true when it comes to recovering from mistakes. By being mindful of our actions, we can catch ourselves before we make a mistake. And if we do make a mistake, mindfulness allows us to see it for what it is - an opportunity to learn and grow. When we are mindful, we are better able to see our mistakes as just that - mistakes. We can learn from them and move on, rather than letting them define us. So next time you find yourself making a mistake, take a deep breath and be mindful of the situation. See it for what it is and use it as an opportunity to learn and grow.

There are many mindful techniques that can help you learn from your mistakes. One is to simply pay attention to your mistakes. Notice what led up to the mistake and what happened afterward. This will help you understand what went wrong and how to avoid making the same mistake again.

Another technique is to accept your mistakes. Don't beat yourself up or dwell on what went wrong. Accept that you made a mistake, and then let it go. This will help you move on from your mistakes more quickly and prevent you from making them again in the future.

Finally, don't be afraid to ask for help when it comes to handling criticism and pressure. Talk to a trusted friend or family member or seek out professional help if you're struggling to cope. Remember, you don't have to go through this alone.

How could you have reacted to your last mistake better?

What actionable steps can you take to react better the next time? (There will be a next time.)

Handling Criticism and Pressure

Handling criticism and pressure is an important part of being an athlete. Not everyone will agree with you or your methods. There will always be people who are critical of what you do. It is important to listen to constructive criticism, but don't let it get to you. Use it as motivation to improve and prove the critics wrong.

What is constructive criticism?

Constructive criticism is a positive way to give feedback that helps improve performance. When delivered effectively, it can motivate and inspire people to do their best work. It should be specific, objective, and focused on the future. The goal is to help the person understand what they need to do differently in order to improve. To be constructive, criticism must be delivered in a way that is respectful and professional. It should never be personal or vague. When given constructively, criticism can be a valuable tool for helping people reach their full potential.

What is negative criticism?

Negative criticism is when someone points out what is wrong with something you have done without offering any helpful advice on how to improve. It can be extremely frustrating, especially if you are trying your best and making an effort to improve. Unfortunately, negative criticism is often unavoidable, especially in competitive sports. However, it is important to remember that not all criticism is bad. In fact, some criticism can be quite helpful if it is constructive and leads to positive change. The key is to be able to differentiate between the two and to use negative criticism as a motivation to improve rather than letting it get you down.

If someone in a position of authority is using negative criticism to hurt people or is making threats, it is important to report it. Talk to a trusted friend or family member about what is going on and ask for their advice. You can also reach out to a professional counselor for help. It is never okay for someone in a position of authority to use their power to hurt or control others. If you are in a situation like this, please reach out for help. There is a resources section at the back of this book with helpful information.

Developing a Healthy Mindset on Criticism

Here are some things that you can do to develop a healthy mindset when it comes to criticism and pressure:

Acknowledge your feelings. It is perfectly normal to feel upset, defensive, or even hurt when you receive criticism. Don't try to bottle up these emotions or pretend they don't exist. Instead, allow yourself to feel them and then let them go. Write them in a journal. Talk to a friend or trusted adult. Find a healthy outlet for those emotions.

Be mindful of your reaction. It is important to be aware of how you react to criticism and pressure. If you find yourself getting defensive or feeling overwhelmed, take a step back and take a few deep breaths. Remember that you have the power to choose how you react to these things.

Focus on the positive. When you receive criticism, try to focus on the positive aspects of it. What can you learn from it? How can it help you improve? What are the potential benefits of taking constructive feedback and using it to your advantage?

Let go of perfection. One of the biggest mistakes that people make is trying to be perfect. Perfect ion is an impossible standard to meet, and it will only lead to frustration and disappointment. Instead of striving for perfection, focus on doing your best and learning from your mistakes.

Seek out support. Finally, don't be afraid to ask for help when it comes to handling criticism and pressure. Talk to a trusted friend or family member or seek out professional help if you feel like you are struggling to cope.

No one likes to be criticized, but it is an inevitable part of being an athlete. The key is to develop a healthy mindset and to use it as motivation to improve. With the right attitude, you can turn criticism into something positive that will help you reach your goals.

It can be difficult to stay positive and motivated when faced with criticism and pressure, but it is important to remember that not all criticism is bad. In fact, some criticism can be quite helpful if it is constructive and leads to positive change. The key is to be able to differentiate between the two and to use negative criticism as a motivation to improve rather than letting it get you down.

Celebrated Olympic gymnast Simone Biles faced tremendous pressure heading into the 2021 Tokyo Olympics. To listen to the news, you would think that the entire fate of the US performance at the Olympics rested on her shoulders.

Biles struggled at the Olympics. She made mistakes. She ended up withdrawing from all of the Olympic events except for two.

One former Olympic gold medalist said Biles needed "to check herself" (Dawson, 2021). British TV host and columnist Piers Morgan called her "selfish" and said she had let down her teammates (Cooper, 2021).

Thankfully, Simone has developed a healthy mindset when it comes to criticism and pressure. She posted on her Instagram account, "I'm proud of myself and the career I've had thus far. This Olympics doesn't erase the past accomplishments I've achieved, nor does it define who I am as an athlete."

Biles placed her trust in her team, stating in a press conference, "I knew that the girls would do an absolutely great job. And I didn't want to risk the team a medal for kind of my screwups because they've worked way too hard for that. So, I just decided that those girls need to go and do the rest of our competition."

She told the Associated Press, "We also have to focus on ourselves because at the end of the day, we're human, too. We have to protect our mind and our body, rather than just go out there and do what the world wants us to do."

Making mistakes and dealing with such harsh criticism on one of the largest stages in the world is no doubt terrifying. But Biles handled everything with grace and positivity. She is an example that anyone can look to for inspiration.

What pressures are you currently facing?

What criticisms are you currently facing?

Are they constructive or negative?

What is your mindset when it comes to criticism and pressure?

What actionable steps can you take to develop a healthy mindset?

Chapter 10: A Healthy Mindset for Balance

Finding a balance between school, work, and play can be difficult. Juggling responsibilities while trying to find time for relaxation seems impossible. However, with a mindful approach, it is possible to find a healthy balance that works for you.

A healthy mindset is all about creating balance. You need to focus on your physical, mental, and emotional health. When you are physically healthy, you have the energy and strength to pursue your goals. When you are mentally healthy, you have the clarity and focus on achieving your dreams. When you are emotionally healthy, you have the courage and confidence to live your life to the fullest.

David Allen, one of the current top productivity gurus, said, "If you don't pay appropriate attention to what has your attention, it will take more of your attention than it deserves" (Allen, 2022).

Look back at your goals from Chapter 4.

What goals did you make that relate to school?

What goals did you make that relate to work?

What goals did you make relating to sports?

What goals are specifically personal goals unrelated to these three areas?

What responsibilities do you have outside of your goals?

As anyone who has ever tried to juggle multiple responsibilities knows, it can be a challenge to keep everything in balance. There are two main ways to approach this task: managing time and managing energy.

Time management involves creating a schedule and sticking to it, which can be difficult when unexpected events pop up. Energy management is a bit more flexible; it involves knowing when to push through and when to take a break. Both approaches have their advantages and disadvantages, so it's important to find the method that works best for you. If you're the type of person who thrives on structure, then time management may be the way to go. But if you're more spontaneous, then energy management may be a better fit. Ultimately, the best way to balance your responsibilities is the way that works best for you.

Time Management

Managing your time can be a difficult task, but it is essential for success in your personal and athletic life. There are a few simple steps that you can take to start managing your time more effectively.

First, make a list of the tasks that you need to accomplish each day. Prioritize the items on your list so that you know which ones are most important. It is a good idea to prioritize responsibilities first. For example, if you need to feed the dog every day before you leave the house, that should be a top priority because the dog can't do that on its own.

Now, allocate a specific amount of time to each task. This will be the amount of time you expect each task to take.

Time Blocking

Time blocking is a strategy that can be used to manage time more effectively. The basic idea is to block off specific periods of time for specific activities. For example, you might block off the first hour of each day for your morning routine, followed by eight hours for school, then an hour after school for practice. You may block out time in the evening for your evening routine and time for work. You can color-code different activities to make things easier to see at a glance. By scheduling your time in this way, you can ensure that you are making the most efficient use of your time.

For example, using time blocking, your schedule might look something like this.

Additionally, time blocking can help to reduce distractions and procrastination, as you will be less likely to wander off-task if you have a set plan for how to use your time.

You can look at space in your schedule and see where you can find time to work towards your goals.

Creating a schedule with free tools such as Google Calendar or iCal can help you create a time-blocked schedule that you can stick to.

Be sure to include breaks in your schedule so that you don't get overwhelmed or burnt out. Finally, stick to your schedule as much as possible and don't try to do too much at once.

Energy Management

Time management doesn't work for everyone. Energy management is another great way to balance your schedule. Our bodies naturally go through cycles of energy throughout the day, and by learning how to identify and work with these natural rhythms, we can greatly improve our focus and efficiency. For example, many people find that they have the most energy in the morning, so they use this time for tasks that require mental focus and concentration. As the day goes on and our energy levels dip, we can switch to less demanding tasks, such as spending time with friends and family or enjoying a hobby.

Start by assigning an energy level to each responsibility. For example, practice will be a high-energy activity, while your morning routine will be a low-energy activity. Then assign energy levels for each of your goals.

Over the next few days, keep track of what energy level you have during unscheduled time and match your typical energy level at that time to a goal with the same energy level.

Downtime is Just as Important as Active Time

As any athlete knows, the key to peak performance is a balance of active and inactive time. While it is important to put in the hard work during practice and training, it is just as important to take time to rest and recover. During downtime, the body has a chance to repair muscle tissue, replenish energy stores, and remove waste products. This is essential for maintaining long-term health and preventing injury. Furthermore, downtime provides an opportunity to mentally recharge, which can help to improve focus and concentration. So next time you're feeling lazy, remember that downtime is just as important as active time. Give yourself a break, and you'll be ready to perform at your best when it matters most.

As anyone who has ever tried to balance their school, work, sports, and personal goals knows, it can be difficult to find the right mix. You may feel like you're constantly juggling tasks and never have enough time for yourself. By creating this visual representation of your days, you can see how much time you're actually spending on each type of activity. You can then begin to make adjustments to your schedule. For example, if you realize that you're working long hours but not taking enough time for yourself, you may decide to cut back on your work hours or take more breaks during the day. By tracking your time and energy, you can gain valuable insights into your daily routine and find ways to create a more balanced schedule.

Chapter 11: Dealing with Injuries and Setbacks

Anyone who has ever played a sport also knows that there will be times when you lose. It's how you deal with those losses that define you as an athlete. The same is true in life. You will have setbacks, but it's how you deal with them that defines you as a person. If you have a healthy mindset, you will see setbacks as opportunities to learn and grow. You will use them to make you stronger and more resilient. You will come out of them better than before.

Dealing with Setbacks

A setback is anything that throws you off your game, whether it's an injury, a loss, or a bad day. It's important to learn how to deal with setbacks because they are a part of life. If you can learn to stay positive and keep moving forward even when things are tough, then you will be successful no matter what.

It's important to have a healthy mindset when dealing with setbacks. Remember that setbacks are temporary, and they don't define you as a person. They are simply opportunities to learn and grow. So, don't let them get you down. Stay positive and keep moving forward.

One of the best ways to deal with a setback is to be mindful of your thoughts and emotions. Don't dwell on what went wrong or how much it stinks. Instead, focus on the present moment and what you can do to improve the situation.

Ashley Wagnor, an Olympic figure skater, said, "Setbacks are inevitable, especially in my sport. Ice is slippery. Life happens. But at the end of the day, you set a goal for yourself. If you can acknowledge that you are not just going to get there in a day and that it takes baby steps along the way, that makes it so much more manageable" (*5 Olympians Share Their Advice for Overcoming Setbacks*, 2018).

Whenever you experience a setback, it's important to take a step back and assess your goals. Are you still on track to achieve what you set out to do? Or do you need to make some adjustments? For example, let's say you're training for a marathon. But then you get injured and have to take several weeks off from running. In this case, you might need to readjust your goal of running the marathon in 3 months. Instead, you might aim to run the marathon in 6 months. The key is not to get discouraged by setbacks. Instead, use them as an opportunity to reassess your goals and make any necessary adjustments.

When it comes to competition, there are always going to be winners and losers. But no matter the outcome, there are always things that you can take away from the experience. For example, if you win, you can take pride in your accomplishments and use them to motivate you to keep pushing yourself. On the other hand, if you lose, you can learn from your mistakes and use them as a springboard for improvement. Either way, it's important to remember that the key to success is always striving to do your best.

What setbacks have you dealt with in the past?

How did you react to those setbacks?

Knowing what you know now about developing a healthy mindset, what can you change in the way you deal with setbacks moving forward?

Dealing with Injuries

Injuries are an unfortunate part of the game. But it's not just the physical pain that can be tough to deal with - the mental toll of an injury can be just as bad, if not worse. The key to recovery is to maintain a healthy mindset. It's important to stay positive and believe that you will make a full recovery. This can be difficult, but it's essential in order to stay motivated and focused on your rehabilitation.

Having a healthy mindset can help athletes deal with injuries and setbacks in a few ways. First, mindfulness can help you stay in the present moment. When you're mindful, you're focused on the here and now rather than worrying about what might happen in the future. This can be helpful when you're dealing with an injury, as it allows you to focus on the healing process rather than worrying about when you'll be able to return to your sport.

A healthy mindset can also help you accept your injury and the setbacks that come with it. Acceptance doesn't mean that you're happy about your injury, but it does mean that you're accepting of the situation and are willing to work through it.

Using Mindfulness to Deal with Injuries and Setbacks

Injuries and setbacks are an unfortunate part of any athlete's career. But how you deal with them can make all the difference. Mindfulness can be a powerful tool for managing pain, boredom, and frustration. Here are some tips for using mindfulness to deal with injuries and setbacks:

Acknowledge your feelings. It's normal to feel disappointed, angry, or sad when you get injured or have a setback. Allow yourself to feel these emotions, but don't dwell on them. Acknowledge them and then let them go.

Be present in the moment. When you're injured or dealing with a setback, it's easy to dwell on what could have been or what might happen in the future. But all that does is add to your stress levels. Instead, focus on the present moment and what you can do right now to help yourself recover.

Don't compare yourself to others. It's natural to compare yourself to other athletes who are healthy and able to train freely. But this only leads to feelings of envy and resentment. Remember that everyone is on their own journey, and comparisons are pointless.

Find things to appreciate. When you're injured or going through a tough time, it can be easy to focus on all the negative things. But there are always things to be grateful for. Maybe you have a great support system, or maybe you're able to use this time to work on other aspects of your life. Whatever it is, find something to appreciate each day.

Aaron Volpatti was never supposed to make it to the NHL. That's what the doctors said after he was severely burned in an accident. But Aaron didn't listen to them. He worked hard in rehabilitation and made it his goal to play professional hockey. And that's exactly what he did.

Aaron was a guest on my Podcast, The Mike Hartman Show, in January 2022. In the summer of 2005, his team had just lost a game, and the whole team went camping. Things got a little out of hand, and Aaron spilled gas on himself – then he caught on fire. Aaron received 2nd, and 3rd-degree burns to 35% of his body (Hartman, 2022, 7:00).

When he woke up in the hospital, he was wrapped like a mummy and thought his career was over (Hartman, 2022, 11:30). But he still had the mindset that he could bounce back and lead a relatively normal life.

He got a call from his coach. A team was looking for a player, and Aaron fit the bill. His coach said, "I need a guy who can put the fear of God into the defensemen of the Ivy League." There was just one problem. He was still recovering in the burn unit (Hartman, 2022, 14:58).

"I hung up the phone, and I just remember crying and getting really emotion like I'd worked my whole life, almost 20 years for that opportunity, and now I'm stuck here, and my career is over," he said (Hartman, 2022, 15:30).

The doctors gave him a long list of reasons why he couldn't play again, but Aaron just made a choice that would not be him, and he got to work.

He said, "Mindset and visualization allowed me to go on this journey to the NHL, but it also saved my life after retirement" (Hartman, 2022, 3:03).

Aaron is an inspiration to all athletes. He shows that with hard work and dedication, anything is possible. Despite the odds, he made it to the NHL and played for several years. He is a role model for anyone who has ever been told they can't achieve their dreams.

Chapter 12: Eating Right, Staying in Shape, and Getting Rest

It can be tough to maintain a balanced lifestyle. Juggling work, family, and social obligations can be a challenge, but it's important to make time for yourself too. To maintain a healthy mindset, you have to eat right, stay in shape, and get enough rest.

The Importance of a Balanced Lifestyle

When it comes to leading a healthy life, balance is key. That means striking a balance between work and play, between rest and activity, and between healthy and unhealthy habits. It can be easy to let one side or the other tip the scales, but when everything is in balance, we feel our best. A balanced lifestyle includes plenty of physical activity to keep our bodies strong and promote cardiovascular health, but it also includes enough rest and relaxation to allow our bodies to repair and recharge. Eating a balanced diet is important, too, ensuring that we get the nutrients we need to function at our best. And finally, maintaining a healthy mental state is essential for overall well-being. When all of these aspects are in balance, we can lead happier, healthier lives.

Maintaining a healthy mindset is essential for leading a healthy lifestyle. When our minds are healthy, we're better able to make positive choices for our bodies and our lives. A healthy mindset allows us to stay positive and motivated, even when things get tough. It helps us to set realistic goals and stay on track, and it gives us the strength to make healthy choices even when we're tempted to veer off course.

If you're looking to live a healthier life, remember that balance is key. Eating right, staying active, and getting enough rest are all important parts of leading a healthy lifestyle. And don't forget the importance of a healthy mindset!

Use a Mind Map

The Hartman.Academy Mind Map is a great tool for athletes of all ages to plan out their goals for mental toughness, physical health, and nutrition. Filling out the numerous fields may seem overwhelming at first, but it is actually fairly simple to complete. The main branches on the mind map are labeled with the different aspects of athletic preparation, while the sub-branches provide more specific details. For example, under the branch labeled "Nutrition," there are sub-branches for "Pre-game Meal," "Supplements," and "Hydration." By filling out the various fields, athletes can develop a comprehensive plan to help them achieve their goals. In addition, the mind map can be used as a reference point throughout the season to ensure that athletes are staying on track. Ultimately, the Hartman.Academy Mind Map is a valuable tool that can help athletes of all ages visualize a plan for success.

There are three main topics in the Hartman.Academy Mind Map: mental toughness, physical, and nutrition. Under physical, you may write "exercise" as a subcategory. Under mental toughness, you may list "visualization techniques" and "positive self-talk" as subcategories. Lastly, under nutrition, you may list "drink more water" and "choose healthy snacks" as subcategories. The great thing about a mind map is it's entirely personal, and there is no right or wrong way to fill it out. The Hartman.Academy Mind Map is essential for all athletes as it creates a plan while minimizing stress and maximizing success on the court, fields, etc.

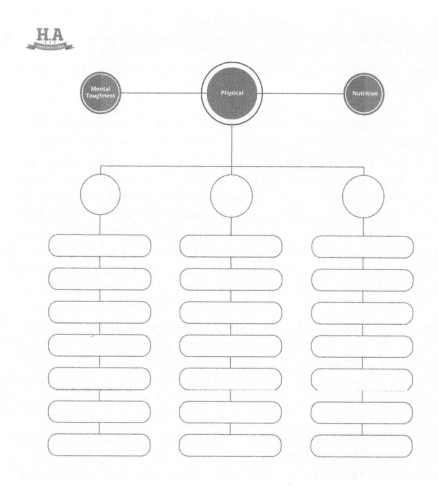

Mental Toughness

Mental toughness is often said to be the key to success. But what exactly is mental toughness? And how can it be developed? Mental toughness can be defined as the ability to remain focused and motivated in the face of adversity. It is about bouncing back from setbacks and having the grit and determination to keep going even when things are tough. So how can mental toughness be developed? One of the most important things is to have a plan. Having a plan gives the mind something to focus on and allows for adaptation if a roadblock occurs. If this happens, the mind needs to be ready to face the challenge and overcome it by being mentally prepared and tough.

Eating Right

Nutrition is often the most overlooked aspect of health for athletes, as there are numerous players who do not properly pay attention to what they consume.

Eating right is about more than just consuming the right nutrients. It's also about creating a healthy mindset. When you make healthy food choices, you're sending a message to your body that you're ready to treat it with respect. Eating right isn't always easy, but it's worth it when you see how much better you feel. When you have more energy and feel less sluggish, it's easier to stick to your workout routine. You'll also find that you have an easier time concentrating and making healthy choices throughout the day. When filling out a mind map, it is crucial to think of possible ways to fuel your body before a game, practice, or tournament in order to reach your maximum potential.

When you eat healthy foods, your body gets the nutrients it needs to function at its best. Eating a balanced diet is important for overall health, and when you fuel your body with nutritious foods, you're doing your part to keep it running smoothly. The benefits of eating healthy foods are many, and they include:

- Increased energy levels
- Improved concentration
- Better digestion
- Stronger immunity
- Healthier body
- Healthier mind
- Reduced risk of developing diseases

What does your typical daily food intake look like?

What is your motivation behind adopting a healthier lifestyle?

Cheryl Buckley, MBA, MS, RDN, LDN, CDN, IFNA COT, is a licensed Registered Dietitian, Food and Nutrition expert dedicated to improving both health and wellness standards within her community. Her personal health journey is what led her to practice Holistic Nutrition. At the age of 30, she suffered from migraines and was diagnosed with an autoimmune disease. She was not happy with the western medicines' approach of just medicating her without getting to the root cause. As a Nutritionist, Cheryl did research and found a practice called Functional Nutritional Medicine – also known as Holistic Nutrition. As a nutritionist, she was intrigued by how the whole-body approach could heal her from the inside out. Cheryl went on to study this practice and became an anti-inflammatory RD who specializes in gut health and immune support using a Mediterranean plant-based diet.

Holistic nutrition focuses on addressing the root cause of your health troubles rather than just masking your symptoms with medications. The first part of the healing process is to remove any obstacles to good health that you may be facing.

Please consult your physician before beginning any meal plan found in this book or any referenced site. Mike Hartman, Hartman.Academy, Echo Net Media, Inc., or any of its affiliates are not responsible for any issues that may result from meal programs from this book. It's important to review each meal program with your physician or a nutritionist before beginning to ensure they are all completed with proper form.

Carbohydrates

Carbohydrates are the body's main source of fuel and should make up 45-65% of your daily caloric intake. Carbohydrates are critical for optimum performance because they are easily converted to glucose, which is used by the muscles for energy. If carbohydrate stores are depleted, blood sugar levels drop and exercise intensity declines.

To maintain optimal carbohydrate stores, eat high-quality carbs prior to exercise and during exercise lasting longer than one hour. During shorter or moderate-intensity exercise, your body can burn fat for fuel; however, you will not be able to perform at your highest level. Therefore, it is essential to consume carbohydrates both before and during exercise to maintain blood sugar levels and exercise intensity.

Recommended daily carbohydrate intake:

When it comes to carbohydrate-rich foods, the Glycemic Index (GI) is a helpful way to rank them according to how they affect blood sugar levels. Foods with a high GI score are more likely to cause a spike in blood sugar, while those with a lower GI score have a less pronounced effect. This is important for people who are trying to manage their blood sugar levels, as well as for athletes who need to maintain energy levels during exercise.

In general, very light training programs (low-intensity or skill-based exercise) require 3-5 grams of carbohydrate per kilogram of body weight, while moderate-intensity programs require 5-7 grams per kilogram. For endurance athletes doing moderate to high-intensity exercise for 1-3 hours per day, 6-10 grams of carbohydrate per kilogram of body weight is recommended. And for those doing moderate to high-intensity exercise for 4-5 hours per day, 8-12 grams per kilogram is recommended. Keeping these guidelines in mind can help you choose the right carb-rich foods to fuel your body before and during exercise.

Some common high-GI foods include white bread, potatoes, and refined breakfast cereal, while some moderate-GI foods include oats and tropical fruits like bananas and mangos.

Low-GI foods include milk, yogurt, lentils, nuts, and fruits like apples, berries, and oranges. In general, it is best to choose foods with a low or moderate GI score in order to maintain stable blood sugar levels throughout the day.

Fiber is a type of complex carb that is particularly important for keeping you feeling full after eating. That's because fiber takes longer to digest than other types of carbs, meaning it stays in the stomach for a longer period of time. This delay in digestive transit can help to control hunger and prevent overeating. Additionally, fiber helps to maintain normal blood sugar levels by slowing the absorption of glucose into the bloodstream. This steadier release of energy can help to keep you feeling energetic throughout the day. Some examples of high-fiber foods are vegetables, fruits and whole grains.

Fiber is also linked with a number of other health benefits, including improved heart health, reduced risk of gastrointestinal disorders, and stronger immunity. Furthermore, fiber plays an important role in metabolism and hormone balance, which can impact mental health.

Protein

As any athlete knows, protein is essential for building muscle and aiding recovery. However, the timing of protein intake is also important. While it is often recommended to consume protein before a workout, this may not be the most effective strategy. Protein is not an efficient energy source, so it will not provide a boost of energy during a workout. Instead, it is best to consume protein after a workout, when the body needs it for recovery.

During exercise, the body breaks down muscle tissue, and protein helps to repair this damage. Protein also plays a role in hormonal balance and metabolism, so it is important to consume enough after a workout in order to support these functions. However, it is important to moderate protein intake, as excessive intake may contribute to dehydration or weight gain.

Recommended protein intake:

The Recommended Dietary Allowance (RDA) for protein is 0.8 grams per kilogram of body weight or about 55 grams per day for the average adult. However, athletes and other highly active individuals may require up to twice as much protein as sedentary people. The best way to ensure adequate protein intake is to eat a varied diet that includes plenty of lean meats, poultry, fish, legumes, nuts, and seeds. For those who are unable to meet their protein needs through diet alone, protein supplements can be a useful addition. However, it is important to speak with a doctor or dietitian before starting any new supplement regimen.

Protein quality is determined by the presence of all essential amino acids (EAAs). Animal-derived proteins, such as milk, eggs, and meat, are complete proteins, meaning they contain all EAAs. Some plant-based proteins, such as soy, quinoa, amaranth, and buckwheat, are also complete proteins. However, most plant-based proteins, such as legumes, grains, nuts and seeds, are generally low in one or more EAAs. As a result, vegans and vegetarians must consume a variety of these foods in order to get all of the EAAs they need. By contrast, animal protein sources provide a complete package of EAAs in each serving. For this reason, animal proteins are generally considered to be of higher quality than plant proteins.

Fat

Fat is an essential nutrient that the body needs in order to function properly. It is a source of energy, and it also helps to support the joints, immunity, and mental health. Fat is also important for recovery from exercise. While the body does need fat, it is important to choose the right types of fat. Plant-based fats and fish-based fats are the best choices because they offer anti-inflammatory benefits. Trans fats and saturated fats should be avoided because they can contribute to inflammation. By choosing the right types of fat, you can improve your overall health and well-being. Some examples of plant based fats could be chia, flax, hemp seeds or walnuts added to a smoothie, Greek yogurt , oatmeal or salads.

Vitamins & Minerals

While we all know that we need to eat nutritious foods to maintain our health, many of us don't realize the important role that vitamins and minerals play in our bodies. These essential nutrients help us to convert the food we eat into energy, and they also play a vital role in cell regeneration, hormone production, and brain function. Without adequate intake of vitamins and minerals, we would quickly become fatigued, our mood would suffer, and our immune system would become compromised.

Hydration

When we think about being physically fit, we often focus on things like muscular strength and cardiovascular endurance. However, it's important to remember that hydration is also a key component of fitness. When our bodies are properly hydrated, we have more energy and our muscles work more efficiently.

On the other hand, even a small amount of fluid loss can have a negative impact on our performance. For example, a 2-3% loss of body water can lead to impaired endurance, while a 3% loss can cause a decrease in metabolism. In addition, fluid loss can make us more susceptible to heat exhaustion and muscle cramping. Therefore, it's important to make sure that we're drinking adequate fluids before, during, and after physical activity in order to maintain optimal fitness levels.

When exercising, it is especially important to stay hydrated in order to prevent the physiologically deleterious effects of dehydration. There is no one fluid-intake recommendation that will suffice for everyone because of the wide diversity of fluid needs of each individual. However, a good rule of thumb is to drink when thirsty and to urinate frequently (every 2-3 hours). Additionally, note urine color and volume to assess hydration status: dark color urine and relatively small amounts are indications of dehydration.

When you sweat, you lose not only water but also electrolytes like sodium and potassium. This can lead to dehydration, which can cause fatigue, cramps, and other problems. To stay properly hydrated, follow these tips:

- For shorter, lower-intensity activities, drink water before, during, and after exercise.
- For longer or more intense activities, sports drinks can be a good option. They replace electrolytes as well as fluid.
- If you're sweating a lot, eat salty foods before exercise or add salt to your sports drink. This will help replace the sodium you'll lose through sweat.
- After exercise, rehydrate by drinking enough fluid to replace what you lost during exercise. You can weigh yourself before and after exercise to get an idea of how much fluid you need to replace.
- If exercising outdoors in the summer heat, you will need more hydration than usual.

If you're looking for a healthy snack to eat before you hit the gym, there are plenty of options to choose from.

- A banana with nut butter is a good source of both carbohydrates and protein, while oats and fruit provide complex carbs that will give you lasting energy.
- Applesauce and almonds offer a balance of carbs and protein, while a brown rice cake with nut butter provides complex carbs and healthy fats.
- Wheat pita with hummus is another option that provides complex carbs and protein, while a sprouted grain bread with fruit preserve is a good choice if you're looking for something lighter.
- A whole-grain waffle with fruit is a great option if you're looking for something quick and easy to eat on the go.

Choosing the right post-workout snack is essential for helping your body recover from exercise and refuel for the rest of the day. A good rule of thumb is to choose a snack that contains both protein and carbohydrates. Protein helps to repair muscle tissue, while carbohydrates provide the body with energy. Here are some tasty and nutritious post-workout snack ideas:

- Low-fat milk (or soy milk) with a fruit smoothie: This refreshing drink provides both protein and carbohydrates, as well as important vitamins and minerals.
- Hard-boiled eggs & tart cherries: This high-protein snack also provides antioxidants that can help reduce muscle soreness.
- Sliced turkey with pineapple: Turkey is a great source of protein, while pineapple provides over 50% of your daily needs for vitamin C.
- Half a turkey sandwich with hummus: This hearty snack will help you refuel after a strenuous workout. The combination of protein, complex carbs, and healthy fats will keep you feeling satisfied until your next meal.
- Sprouted grain bread & peanut butter: Peanut butter is a good source of protein and healthy fats, while sprouted grain bread provides complex carbs and fiber.
- Tuna salad with avocado on whole-wheat bread: This filling snack provides a balance of protein, healthy fats, and complex carbs (Buckley, 2022).

Take some time to plan out a week of meals and snacks using the template on the next page. Having a plan will help you stay on track and eat mindfully. Repeating this process each week will help you make healthier choices and plan ahead to have healthy snacks on hand for when cravings hit.

	Breakfast	Lunch	Dinner	Snacks
Monday				
Tuesday				
Wednesday				
Thursday				
Friday				
Saturday				
Sunday				

Staying in Shape

When it comes to physical health, sleep, exercise, strength, and endurance are all important factors to consider. Athletes need to make sure they are getting enough sleep each night, and that their workouts are structured and disciplined in order to see results. Make sure to consider these factors when filling out your mind map.

The definition of fitness is the ability to recover from stress. This is all done through exercise training. The body is constantly bombarded with stress, whether it's from physical activity, mental stress, or environmental toxins. Over time, this stress takes a toll on the body and can lead to fatigue, aches and pains, and even injuries. Fitness training helps to reverse the effects of stress by providing the body with the specific exercises it needs to function optimally. As a result, fitness becomes less about working out hard and more about working out smart. When the body is able to recover from stress more efficiently, it becomes easier to maintain healthy levels of fitness and prevent injuries.

As a former professional athlete, I learned the importance of:

- Having a plan
- Sticking to the plan
- Having a coach or trainer

The fitness program provided here is my personal 3-month training program. While this program may be appropriate for all fitness levels, from beginner to advanced, you must consult your own physician to ensure this program is appropriate for your current fitness level. Each workout is a minimum of 30 minutes and a maximum of 60 minutes.

It is important to always stretch upon completion of your training sessions. Stretching helps to keep muscles long, lean, and healthy. It also helps to prevent injuries by keeping the muscles strong and flexible. However, it is important to never stretch cold muscles before training. Cold muscles are more likely to be injured during stretching. Instead, take a few minutes to warm up the muscles before stretching. This can be done by doing some light cardio or by using a foam roller. Once the muscles are warm, they will be more pliable and less likely to be injured during stretching.

For more guidance and some great tips on stretching, visit Aly Faber, LMBT, CBP, CMP, E-RYT and YACEP, at thestretchlady.com.

The Stretch Lady is a virtual online coaching program for all athletic skill levels, designed to maximize performance in minimum time. Demonstrated by current student-athletes, the format makes it easy and fun to stretch your way towards better overall athletic ability, mobility, injury prevention, recovery, and maximum regeneration. The program includes customized routines based on your individual needs, as well as access to a library of pre-recorded stretching videos.

In addition, the Stretch Lady provides tips and tricks for incorporating stretching into your everyday life, so you can stay flexible and agile no matter what your schedule looks like. Whether you're a seasoned athlete or just getting started on your fitness journey, the Stretch Lady can help you reach your peak performance.

Important Information before Beginning Your Fitness Training Program:

Please consult your physician before beginning any exercise program found in this book or any referenced site. Mike Hartman, Hartman.Academy, Echo Net Media, Inc., or any of its affiliates are not responsible for any injury that may result from exercises or training programs from this book. It's important to review each program and exercise with your physician and or/trainer before beginning to ensure they are all completed with proper form.

Body Weight Training – Monday / Wednesday / Friday

Each training session should start with a dynamic warm up and consists of 4 sets of 3 different exercise routines. Each set is repeated 4 times. Measure your improvement based on how many total repetitions you complete:

- Beginner: 10 repetitions / exercise = 480 total repetitions

- Getting Serious: 15 repetitions / exercise = 720 total repetitions
- Advanced: 20 repetitions / exercise = 960 repetitions
- Ultimate Challenge: 25 repetitions / exercise = 1,200 repetitions

Aerobic / Anaerobic Training – Tuesday / Thursday / Saturday

Choose from any of the Aerobic activities and follow this approach:

- Dynamic Warm-up: 30 minutes (Baseline)
- Interval: 30 seconds high intensity / 30 seconds recovery.
- Repeat for 10 / 20 / 30 minutes depending on fitness level
- Recovery: 10 minutes easy pace

Activities:

Recumbent Bike	Elliptical	Walking
Jump Rope	Boxing	Swimming
Seated Bike	Cycling	Jump Rope
Stair Climber	Running	Dancing

Record your repetitions for each exercise/activity to chart your progress.

Month 1

BODY WEIGHT TRAINING

	Exercise 1				Exercise 2				Exercise 3			
Set 1	Standard Push-Up				Wall Squats w/ Ball				Double Crunch			
MONDAY												
WEDNESDAY	1	2	3	4	1	2	3	4	1	2	3	4
FRIDAY												

	Exercise 1				Exercise 2				Exercise 3			
Set 2	Dive Bomber Push-Up				Lateral Squat				Air Bike Crunches			
MONDAY												
WEDNESDAY	1	2	3	4	1	2	3	4	1	2	3	4
FRIDAY												

	Exercise 1				Exercise 2				Exercise 3			
Set 3	Diamond Push-Up				Hamstring Curl				Alternating Superman			
MONDAY												
WEDNESDAY	1	2	3	4	1	2	3	4	1	2	3	4
FRIDAY												

	Exercise 1				Exercise 2				Exercise 3			
Set 4	Close Grip Push-Up				Stability Ball Pull-In				Upright Row w/ Bands			
MONDAY												
WEDNESDAY	1	2	3	4	1	2	3	4	1	2	3	4
FRIDAY												

AEROBIC / ANAEROBIC TRAINING

	Actvitiy	Minutes
TUESDAY		
THURSDAY		
SATURDAY		

Month 2

BODY WEIGHT TRAINING

	Exercise 1	Exercise 2	Exercise 3
Set 1	Bench Press w/ Bands	Alternating Lunges	Rugby Crunches
MONDAY			
WEDNESDAY			
FRIDAY			

	Exercise 1	Exercise 2	Exercise 3
Set 2	Front Raises w/ Bands	Squat Jumps (Low Impact)	Plank (60 Seconds)
MONDAY			
WEDNESDAY			
FRIDAY			

	Exercise 1	Exercise 2	Exercise 3
Set 3	Plyo Push-Up from Knees	Sumo Squat	Toe Touches
MONDAY			
WEDNESDAY			
FRIDAY			

	Exercise 1	Exercise 2	Exercise 3
Set 4	Arm Curls w/ Bands	Hamstring Touches	Side Plank (30 Seconds)
MONDAY			
WEDNESDAY			
FRIDAY			

AEROBIC / ANAEROBIC TRAINING

	Actvitiy	Minutes
TUESDAY		
THURSDAY		
SATURDAY		

Month 3

BODY WEIGHT TRAINING

	Exercise 1	Exercise 2	Exercise 3

Set 1 — Close Grip Push-Up / Sumo Squat / Plank (60 Seconds)

	1	2	3	4	1	2	3	4	1	2	3	4
MONDAY												
WEDNESDAY												
FRIDAY												

Set 2 — Bench Press w/ Bands / Lateral Squat / Standing Air Bike

	1	2	3	4	1	2	3	4	1	2	3	4
MONDAY												
WEDNESDAY												
FRIDAY												

Set 3 — Up Right Row w/ Bands / Reverse Lunge / Alternating Superman

	1	2	3	4	1	2	3	4	1	2	3	4
MONDAY												
WEDNESDAY												
FRIDAY												

Set 4 — Standard Push-Up / Leg Extensions w/ Ball / Roll Out w/ Ball

	1	2	3	4	1	2	3	4	1	2	3	4
MONDAY												
WEDNESDAY												
FRIDAY												

AEROBIC / ANAEROBIC TRAINING

	Actvitiy	Minutes
TUESDAY		
THURSDAY		
SATURDAY		

Getting Enough Rest

Getting enough rest is essential for any athlete who wants to perform at their best. When you're well-rested, your body is able to repair damaged muscles, replenish energy stores, and reduce inflammation. Lack of sleep, on the other hand, can lead to fatigue, poor recovery, and increased risk of injury.

When you don't get enough sleep, it can have a major impact on your health. Studies have shown that not sleeping significantly affects your immune system, making you more susceptible to sickness. It can also make you feel overwhelmed with anxiety and depression, as well as decrease your memory and focus. In addition, there is an increased risk of developing heart disease, diabetes, cancer, and other health problems. If you're trying to lose weight, not getting enough sleep can make it harder to reach your goals. That's why it's important to get enough rest every night.

Cheryl Buckley says a good night's sleep is essential for optimal health and performance. Most people need between 7-8 hours of sleep in order to function at their best. The first half of sleep, known as deep sleep, is when our bodies are able to heal and detoxify. This is when our cells repair themselves, and we detox from the day's activities. The second half of sleep, REM sleep, is when our minds start to refresh. This is when we dream, and our memories are consolidated. REM sleep is important for learning and memory formation. A lack of deep or REM sleep can lead to fatigue, irritability, and decreased performance.

Tips for Improving Sleep

Sleep is essential for both our physical and mental well-being. It allows our bodies to heal and repair and our minds to rest and rejuvenate. Yet, according to the National Sleep Foundation, nearly one-third of Americans don't get enough sleep. If you're struggling to get a good night's sleep, Cheryl has suggested some things you can do to improve the quality of your sleep.

It's important to create a routine. Go to bed and get up at the same time each day, and prepare for sleep by doing things like taking a warm bath or meditating. You should also create an environment that is conducive to sleep by keeping the noise and light levels down and maintaining a comfortable temperature. Regular exercise can also help improve sleep. Exercising too late in the day, however, is stimulating and can keep you awake. Finally, avoid napping during the day if you have trouble falling asleep at night, as this can lead to sleep deprivation. If you do need a nap, it's best to keep the nap to 30 minutes or less.

Unfortunately, many people find it difficult to get the rest they need due to stress. Thankfully, there are a number of things that can be done to reduce stress and improve sleep. For instance, it is important to balance work, family and personal time, as well as to establish priorities. It is also helpful to give oneself time to relax throughout the day and to set realistic goals. Additionally, journaling and using relaxation techniques can be very beneficial (Hartman, 2022).

Dr. David Mefford shared a technique for reducing stress and mindfulness with me many years ago called the Gold Paint Theory. This is a visualization practice that can help you be in the moment, be aware of situations, and overcome anything from butterflies before a game to improving the quality of your sleep.

Here's how it works: Go into a quiet place and imagine you have a thick coat of gold paint on your skin from head to toe. Your skin can't breathe with all that paint. Close your eyes and slowly imagine that gold paint coming off your body while using breathing techniques. If your thoughts begin to wander, come back to the paint. Don't move too quickly. Slow down. Be mindful. Be in the moment. Be fully present. The more you practice this technique, the better you will become. It's used by many top athletes to calm down, relax, and just be in the moment.

Tips for Maintaining a Balanced Lifestyle

Achieving a balanced lifestyle is essential for optimal health and well-being. However, it can be difficult to strike the right balance between work, play, and rest. Here are a few tips to help you maintain a healthy lifestyle:

First, make sure to schedule time for physical activity. It doesn't matter what type of exercise you do, as long as you get your heart rate up and break a sweat for at least 30 minutes a day. Regular exercise has countless benefits, including reducing stress levels, improving sleep quality, and boosting energy levels.

Second, eat healthy foods and stay hydrated. Fueling your body with nutritious foods helps your mind and body to function at their best. And don't forget to drink plenty of water! Staying properly hydrated is crucial for maintaining overall health.

Finally, take some time each day to relax and de-stress. Whether it's reading your favorite book, taking a yoga class, or going for a walk in nature, find an activity that helps you to unwind and clear your mind. Giving yourself regular breaks from the hustle and bustle of everyday life is essential for maintaining a balanced lifestyle.

How to Make Time for Yourself

It can be hard to make time for yourself when you're always on the go. But just like it's important to refuel your car's gas tank, it's important to refuel your body and mind too to maintain a healthy mindset. Here are some tips for making time for yourself amidst a busy schedule.

First, try to wake up a little earlier each day and use that extra time to do something that you enjoy. Maybe you can read a book, take a walk outside, or meditate for a few minutes.

Secondly, try to schedule some 'me time' each week. This can be anything from getting a massage to taking a yoga class. And lastly, don't be afraid to say 'no' sometimes. If you're always saying 'yes' to others, you'll never have time for yourself. If someone asks you to do something that you don't really have time for, it's okay to say 'no.'

Making time for yourself is important for your health and well-being, so make it a priority!

Chapter 13: Life After Sports

When you're a young athlete, it's all about the sport. You eat, breathe, and sleep the sport. It's your life. But what happens when that chapter ends? How do you go from being an athlete to becoming a regular person again? It can be tough to make the transition, but with the right mindset and goal setting, it can be done!

Having a Healthy Mindset is Essential When Transitioning Out of Sports

It's important to remember that your worth as a person doesn't come from your athletic ability. You are so much more than just an athlete. It can be easy to forget this when your entire life has revolved around sports, but it's important to remember that there is more to life than just sports.

One of the most difficult things about transitioning out of sports is having to give up the competitive outlet that you're used to. For many athletes, their sport is a way to blow off steam and release pent-up energy. When you're no longer playing sports, it's important to find a new outlet for that energy. Some people find that running or working out is a good way to release pent-up energy, while others may enjoy painting or hiking. It's important to find an activity that you enjoy, and that helps you relieve stress. You may even be able to find a league organized by the community or your workplace that will allow you to continue competing in a sport you love.

Setting Goals in Other Areas of Life

One of the best ways to make the transition is to set goals for yourself in different areas of your life. This will help keep you motivated and on track.

Some goal ideas for different areas of your life include:

- Career: Set a goal to get a promotion or earn a new certification.

- Family: Set a goal to spend more time with your family.

- Personal: Set a goal to eat healthily, save money, or run a half marathon.

- Spiritual: Set a goal to be more mindful in spiritual practice.

No matter what goals you set for yourself, it's important to remember that you are capable of accomplishing anything you set your mind to. Just because you're no longer an athlete doesn't mean you can't achieve great things!

All of the exercises in this workbook apply to every area of life. If you ever feel stuck or have lost momentum, pull out this workbook and redo the self-assessment. It is a good idea to revisit the self-assessment annually (or more often) to reevaluate where you are and where you want to go. Your goals will change throughout your life, and what was once a good goal may no longer be relevant.

The bottom line is that you can do anything you set your mind to. You are not defined by your athletic ability, and there is more to life than just sports. With the right mindset and goalsetting, you can transition from sports to life seamlessly!

What other goals could you set for yourself in different areas of your life?

Staying Motivated When You Aren't Playing Sports

Find a new competitive outlet: Join or form a team with friends to compete in a sport or activity that you enjoy. This can help keep you motivated and allow you to continue enjoying the competition that comes with playing sports.

Find a support system: Family and friends can be a great support system when you're making a transition in your life. They can help you stay motivated and on track.

Remember your worth: You are so much more than just an athlete. Remembering this can help you stay motivated and focused on the other areas of your life that are important to you.

What are some other ways that you could stay motivated when you don't have a sport to focus on?

Finding New Hobbies and Interests Outside of Sports

One of the best things about transitioning out of sports is that you have more time to explore new hobbies and interests. This can be a great opportunity to try something new that you've always wanted to do.

Some ideas for new hobbies and interests include:

- Pick up a musical instrument

- Learn a new language

- Take up painting or photography

- Join a book club, recreational league, or play in pick-up games

- Start a blog or vlog

- Volunteer for a cause that you're passionate about

- Start a business

The sky is the limit when it comes to new hobbies and interests. The important thing is to find something that you enjoy, and that helps you stay motivated.

What other hobbies and interests would you like to explore?

Transitioning from sports to life can be a difficult process, but it is so important to remember that you are capable of so much more than just playing sports. You have so much to offer the world, and there is no one else like you. With the right mindset and goal setting, you can make the transition seamlessly!

Chapter 14: Play to Win

Life is a game. We are all players, and the only way to win is to play to win. But what does that mean? It means being mindful of our actions and not reacting out of anger or jealousy. It means wishing others well and striving to be our best selves. It means being in harmony with ourselves and embracing the journey that life has in store for us.

What is Playing to Win?

For athletes, playing to win means being focused and determined to achieve the desired outcome. It requires complete dedication to the game and a refusal to give up. In order to play to win, athletes must be in control of their own thoughts and emotions, as well as their physical movements. The ability to control one's thoughts and emotions is what separates good athletes from great ones.

Great athletes are able to block out distractions and keep their minds focused on the task at hand. They refuse to let their emotions get the best of them, and they always maintain a level head. Similarly, great athletes are also in complete control of their bodies. They execute each movement with precision, and they have total confidence in their abilities. Playing to win requires that athletes be in complete control of themselves, both mentally and physically. Those who can achieve this state of mind and body are the ones who find success on the playing field.

In life, playing to win means setting and achieving goals. It means taking action instead of reacting to circumstances. And it means always striving to be your best self. When you play to win in life, you are one with yourself. You are focused and dedicated to achieving your goals. And you refuse to let anything or anyone stand in your way. You know that the only person you need to beat is yourself. And so, you strive each and every day to become a better version of yourself.

You challenge yourself to push harder, to go further, and never settle for anything less than your absolute best. Because when you play to win in life, that's exactly what it takes. There are no shortcuts. There are no easy paths. There is only hard work, determination, and never-ending dedication to becoming the best that you can be. So, if you want to win in life, start by setting some goals. Then put in the work required to achieve them. And finally, never give up on yourself. Because when you do, that's when you truly start playing to win.

So, what does it mean to play to win? It means that you are the one in control of your life. You decide what you want to achieve, and then you go out and make it happen. It means being focused and dedicated to your goals and never letting anything stand in your way. It means always striving to be your best self and never settling for anything less. So, if you want to win in life, start by playing to win. Be the game, and never let anyone

I used to think that in order to win in life, you had to be the best at everything you did. I used to think that if I wasn't first, then I was a failure. But I've since learned that this isn't true. In fact, I've learned that trying to be the best at everything is a surefire way to guarantee that you'll never achieve anything. Because the truth is, there will always be someone who is better than you. There will always be someone who is faster, stronger, smarter, or more talented. And that's okay.

What's important is that you don't let those people stop you from trying to be the best that you can be. Just because someone else may be better than you doesn't mean that you can't still be great. So don't strive to be the best; strive to be a little bit better. Strive to be your best self. And when you do that, you'll find that life is much more rewarding.

Focus on Your Healthy Mindset

When you're trying to improve your life and achieve success, it's important to focus on your mindset. Your mindset is the key to everything. It's the difference between achieving your goals and never even getting started. If you want to win in life, you need to have a healthy mindset. You need to be positive and believe in yourself. You need to be willing to work hard and never give up. And most importantly, you need to be mindful of the messages you're sending yourself.

Your mindset is the key to everything. It's the difference between achieving your goals and never even getting started. A positive mindset is essential for success in any endeavor, whether it's losing weight, starting a business, or simply getting out of bed in the morning. Without a positive mindset, it's all too easy to talk yourself out of taking action or giving up when things get tough. But with a positive mindset, anything is possible.

This workbook has guided you through the process of putting together all of the pieces you need to play the game. But it's up to you to take action and make it happen. It's time to start believing in yourself and making things happen. So, get out there and start playing to win!

Resources

Aly Faber: The Stretch Lady, LMBT, CBP, CMP, E-RYT and YACEP: Specializing in Bodywork, Assisted Stretching, Yoga-Based Stretch and Life Coaching thestretchlady.com

Cheryl Buckley, MBA, MS, RDN, LDN, CDN, IFNA COT: Licensed and Registered Dietician and Nutritionist cherylbuckley.com

Center for Young Women's Health and Young Men's Health: These websites provide guides on emotional health, including test anxiety, depression, bullying, and eating disorders. www.youngwomenshealth.org and www.youngmenshealthsite.org

Go Ask Alice!: Geared at young adults, this question-and-answer website contains a large database of questions about a variety of concerns surrounding emotional health. www.goaskalice.columbia.edu

Girls Health.Gov: The "Your Feelings" section of this website offers guidance to teenage girls on recognizing a mental health problem, getting help, and talking to parents. http://girlshealth.gov/feelings/index.html

Jed Foundation: Promoting emotional health and preventing suicide among college students - This website provides an online resource center, **ULifeline**, a public dialogue forum, **Half of Us**, and **Transition Year**, resources and tools to help students transition to college. http://www.jedfoundation.org/students

Reach Out: This website provides information on specific mental health disorders, as well as resources to help teens make safe plans when feeling suicidal and helpful tips on how to relax. http://au.reachout.com/

Teens Health: Providing a safe place for teens who need honest and accurate information, this website provides resources on mental health issues. http://teenshealth.org/teen/your_mind/

Teen Mental Health: Geared towards teenagers, this website provides learning tools on a variety of mental illnesses, videos, and resources for friends. http://teenmentalhealth.org/

Strength of Us: An online community designed to inspire young adults impacted by mental health issues to think positive, stay strong and achieve goals through peer support and resource sharing. http://strengthofus.org/

Helplines

Campaign Against Living Miserably (CALM): Visit www.thecalmzone.net

Crisis Text Line: Visit www.crisistextline.org/ or Text "START" to 741-741

List of International Suicide Hotlines: Visit www.suicide.org/international-suicide-hotlines.html

Love is Respect: Visit www.loveisrespect.org/, text "LOVEIS" to 22522, or call 1-866-331-9474 to talk with a peer advocate to prevent and end abusive relationships

National Eating Disorder Association: Visit www.nationaleatingdisorders.org/ or call 1-800-931-2237

National Suicide Prevention Lifeline: Visit www.suicidepreventionlifeline.org/ or call 1-800-273-TALK (8255)

References

5 Olympians Share Their Advice for Overcoming Setbacks. (2018, February 7). Health. Retrieved May 14, 2022, from https://www.health.com/fitness/olympics-2018-athletes-lolo-jones-ashley-wagner-advice-setbacks

Allen, D. (2002). Getting Things Done: The Art of Stress-Free Productivity (Reprint ed.). Penguin Books.

Allen, K. U. T. (2019, May 27). Love him or hate him, Bruins super-pest Brad Marchand always gets results. USA TODAY. Retrieved May 2, 2022, from https://eu.usatoday.com/story/sports/nhl/columnist/kevinallen/2019/05/27/stanley-cup-2019-brad-marchand-bruins-hated-man/1207184001/

C. Buckley (personal communication, May 25, 2022)

Clear, J. (2018). Atomic Habits: An Easy & Proven Way to Build Good Habits & Break Bad Ones (Illustrated ed.). Avery.

Cooper, S. (2021, July 29). A CNN host roasted Piers Morgan for his attack on Simone Biles and said his only athletic feat is running off his own TV show. Insider. Retrieved May 14, 2022, from https://www.insider.com/piers-morgan-roasted-by-cnn-host-for-simone-biles-criticism-2021-7

Dawson, A. (2021, August 2). Simone Biles "really needs to check herself," according to a former Olympic gold medalist. Insider. Retrieved May 14, 2022, from https://www.insider.com/simone-biles-really-needs-to-check-herself-henry-cejudo-says-2021-8

Dweck, C. S. (2022). MINDSET: NEW PSYCHOLOGY OF SUCCESS. Ballantine Books.

Hartman, M. (2022, March 18). 11. Healthy Mindset For Athletes"Why Sleep is crucial with Cheryl Buckley Part 1". Hartman.Academy. Retrieved June 5, 2022, from https://www.hartman.academy/post/11-athletes-ready-to-play-why-sleep-is-crucial

Hartman, M. (Host). (2022, January 7). On Fire to NHL Aaron Volpatti [Audio podcast episode]. In The Mike Hartman Show. Audible. https://www.audible.com/pd/On-Fire-To-NHL-Aaron-Volpatti-Podcast/B09PY76T79

Kabat-Zinn, J. (2003). Mindfulness-based interventions in context: Past, present, and future. *Clinical Psychology: Science and Practice*, *10*(2), 144–156. https://doi.org/10.1093/clipsy.bpg016

Manon Rhéaume – the first woman to play in an American men's pro sports league. (2021, January 7). Sports Retriever. Retrieved May 7, 2022, from https://www.sportsretriever.com/hockey/manon-rheaume-first-woman-play-american-mens-pro-sports-league/

McKeown, G. (2022). Essentialism: The Disciplined Pursuit of Less. Virgin Books.

Radvillas, H. (2020, October 30). 4 Real Examples of Great Teamwork. TrueSport. Retrieved May 14, 2022, from https://truesport.org/teamwork/four-real-examples-of-great-teamwork/

Rooks, J. D. (2017, April 6). *"We Are Talking About Practice": the Influence of Mindfulness vs. Relaxation Training on Athletes' Attention and Well-Being over High-Demand Intervals*. SpringerLink. Retrieved April 25, 2022, from https://link.springer.com/article/10.1007/s41465-017-0016-5?error=cookies_not_supported&code=b9aef8e1-8a9d-4dd4-82a4-57e78c9bd559

S. Greenapple (personal communication, May 25, 2022)

Sarkar, M., Fletcher, D., & Brown, D. J. (2015). What doesn't kill me. . .: Adversity-related experiences are vital in the development of superior Olympic performance. Journal of Science and Medicine in Sport, 18(4), 475–479. https://doi.org/10.1016/j.jsams.2014.06.010

Smith, M. (2022, April 6). Mark Messier on leadership, trust and magic mushrooms. Macleans.Ca. Retrieved May 7, 2022, from https://www.macleans.ca/longforms/mark-messier-on-leadership-trust-and-magic-mushrooms/

Stillman, J. (2021, January 5). Serena Williams's Secret for Never Cracking Under Pressure Can Work for You, Too. Inc.Com. Retrieved May 2, 2022, from https://www.inc.com/jessica-stillman/steal-serena-williams-mind-trick-for-staying-calm-in-incredibly-stressful-situations.html

Todd Elik. (n.d.). The Hockey History Blog. Retrieved May 7, 2022, from http://lakingslegends.blogspot.com/2010/01/todd-elik.html

Valentine, M. (2019, November 1). *23 Michael Phelps Quotes to Unlock the Champion Within*. Goalcast. https://www.goalcast.com/23-michael-phelps-quotes-unlock-champion-within/

What Is This Thing Called Mental Toughness? An Investigation of Elite Sport Performers. (2010, November 30). Taylor & Francis. Retrieved April 25, 2022, from https://www.tandfonline.com/doi/abs/10.1080/10413200290103509

Acknowledgments

Bob Langley is a former hockey player and corporate trainer who took me in at 16 years old when I moved to Toronto. My first day on the ice, I made the team, and he went to the coach and said he was going to take me under his wing. I moved in with his family. He was like a big brother to me and helped me daily in all areas of my life. To this day, I still go to Bob for advice in my life and business as he has a Ph.D. in life. After 39 years, we still talk weekly. He was at my first game in Maple Leaf Gardens when I played the Toronto Maple Leafs, and he's been there for me ever since. I don't think I would've made it to the next level if I hadn't taken the route that I did and had Bob to help me along the way.

Marty Quarters and I have known each other since we were seven years old. He is from my hometown of Oak Park, Michigan. Marty was always there for me as a good friend and would help me on the ice by doing drills and making sure I was ready for training camp. He also traveled to many stadiums to see me on the road. It was always great to have a friend there to share stories with. There's no doubt he was one of my biggest supporters, and he was always direct with me whether I played a good game or a bad game.

I also want to thank the people who have supported me throughout my life. First and foremost, I want to thank my mother and father, Cheri and John Hartman. They have always been my biggest fans, and I know that I can always count on them for love and support. I also want to thank my brother and sister Michele Coblin and Ricky Hartman and my uncle Sherman Laxer. He has been a great role model for me, and I am grateful for all the advice and wisdom he has shared with me over the years. Finally, I want to thank my daughter Gabrielle and son Chase. They are my pride and joy, and I am so grateful to have them in my life. Words cannot express how thankful I am for all the love and support of these special people in my life.

I would like to say a special thank you to Lindsey Chastain of The Writing Detective (writingdetective.com) for her guidance and assistance in writing this book.

About the Author

Mike Hartman is an American former professional ice hockey player who played 17 years of professional hockey and was a member of the New York Rangers Stanley Cup winning team.

He played in 397 games in the National Hockey League (NHL) for the Buffalo Sabres, Winnipeg Jets, Tampa Bay Lightning, and New York Rangers and played for his country Team USA & the minor leagues.
He was drafted in the seventh round, 131st overall, by the Sabres in the 1986 NHL Entry Draft. In 1995 he was inducted into the Michigan Jewish Sports Hall of Fame and in was inducted into the National Jewish Sports Hall of Fame and Museum.

Throughout his career as a professional hockey player, he benefited from having great coaches and mentors. Combined with his strong drive to improve his game no matter what it took, those coaches and mentors were able to make him a better hockey player and a better man.
Once he retired from hockey, he started looking around for a fulfilling career to take the place of professional sports. He realized he had a real obligation to pay forward the incredible guidance he received when he was growing up and during his career.

He established the Hartman.Academy to work with athletes, workplace athletes, coaches and anyone who wants to get better at what they do.

Made in the USA
Middletown, DE
24 August 2024

59122333R00064